Wonderful Mandala Patterns Coloring

Copyright: Published in the United States by Nancy McCowan
Published January 2017
ISBN-13: 978-1542632317
ISBN-10: 1542632315

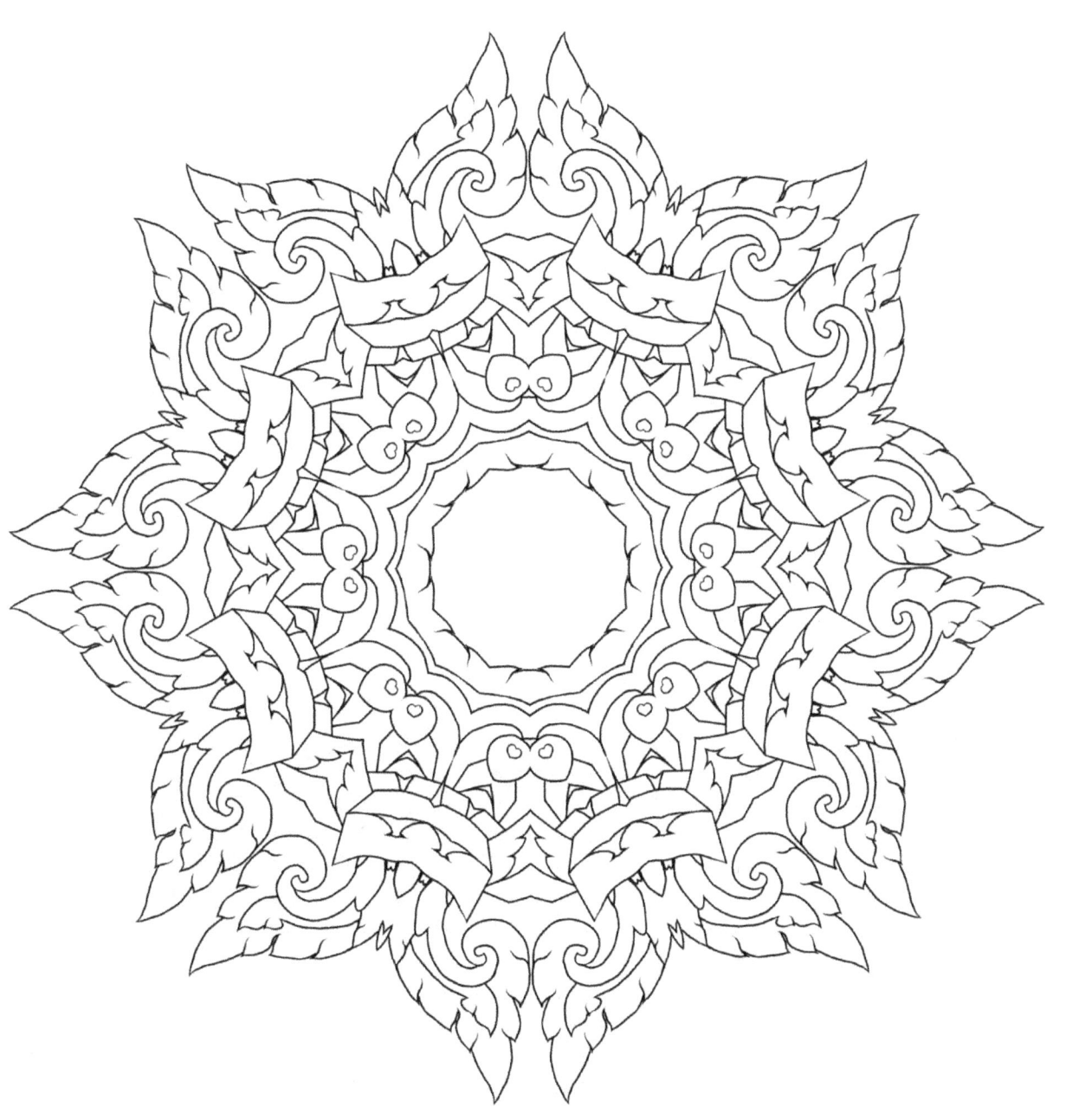

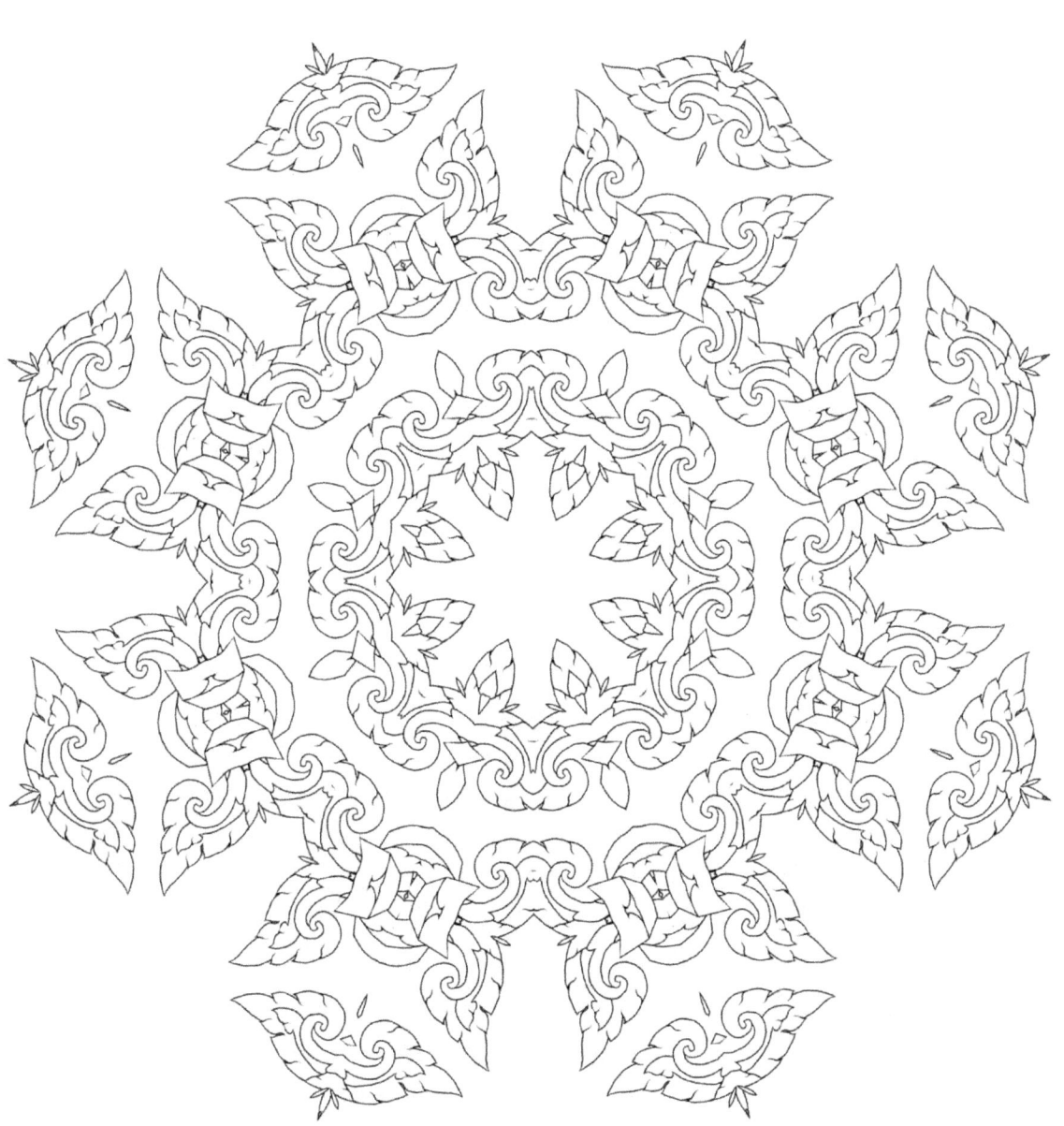

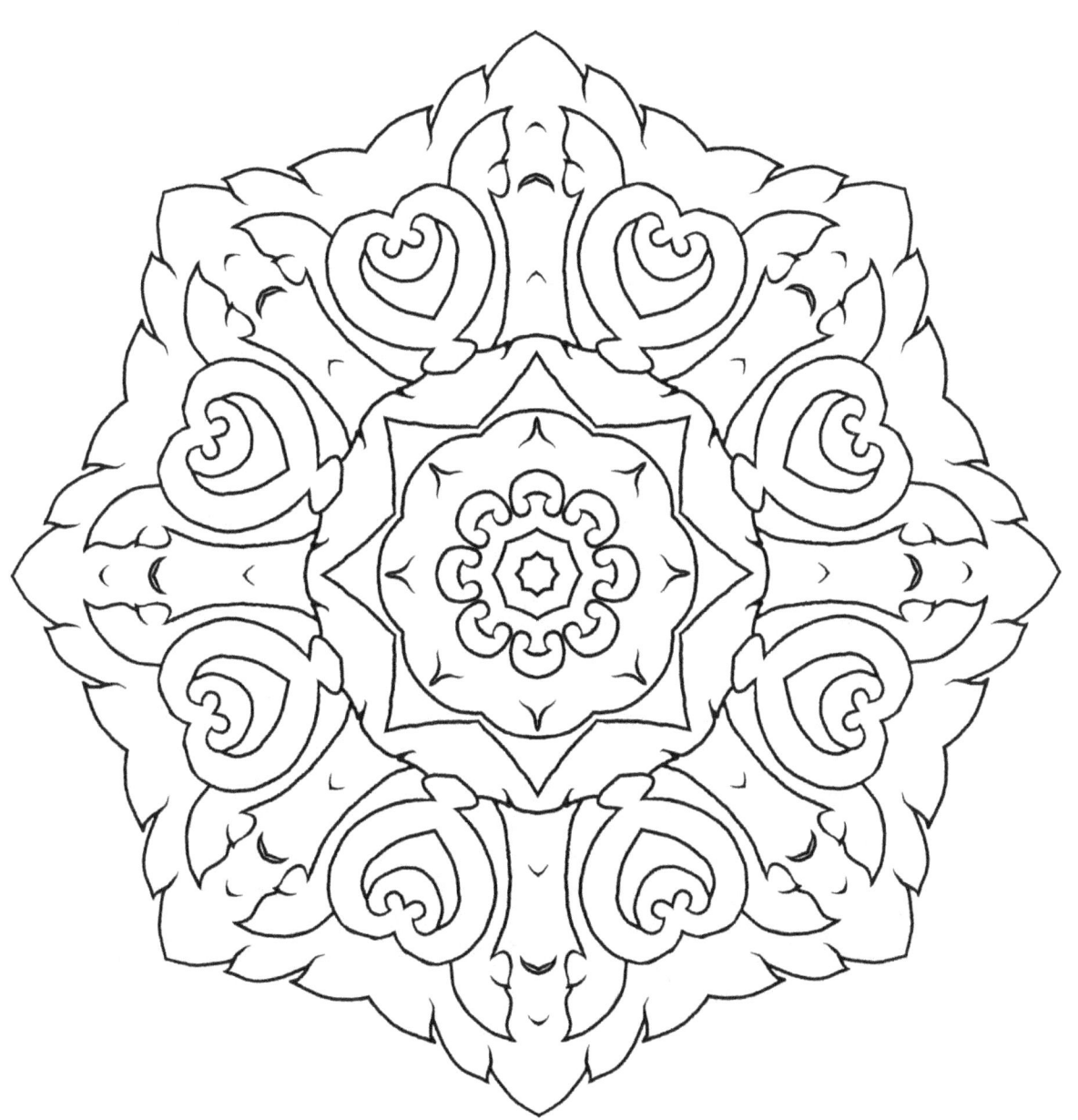

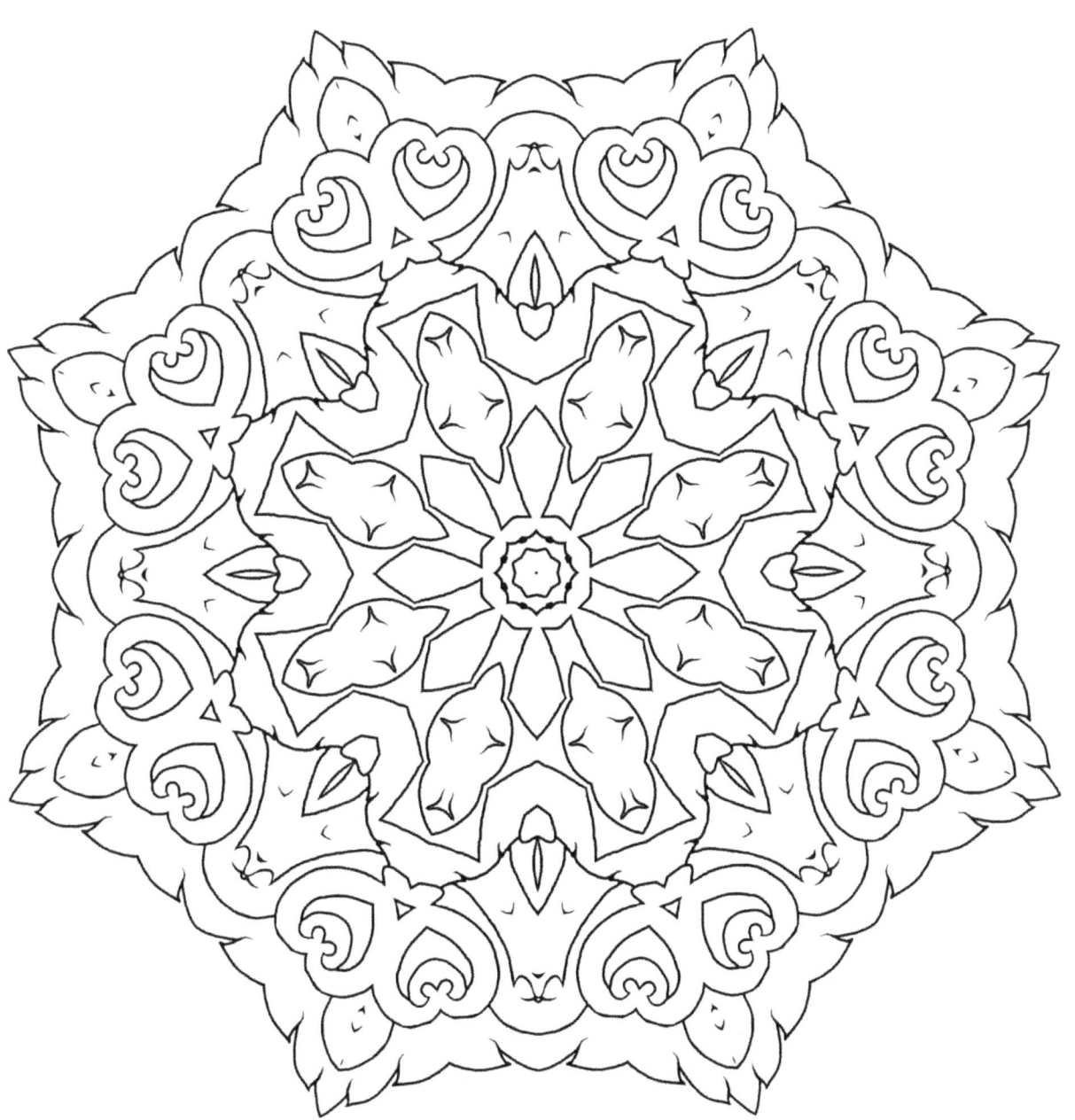

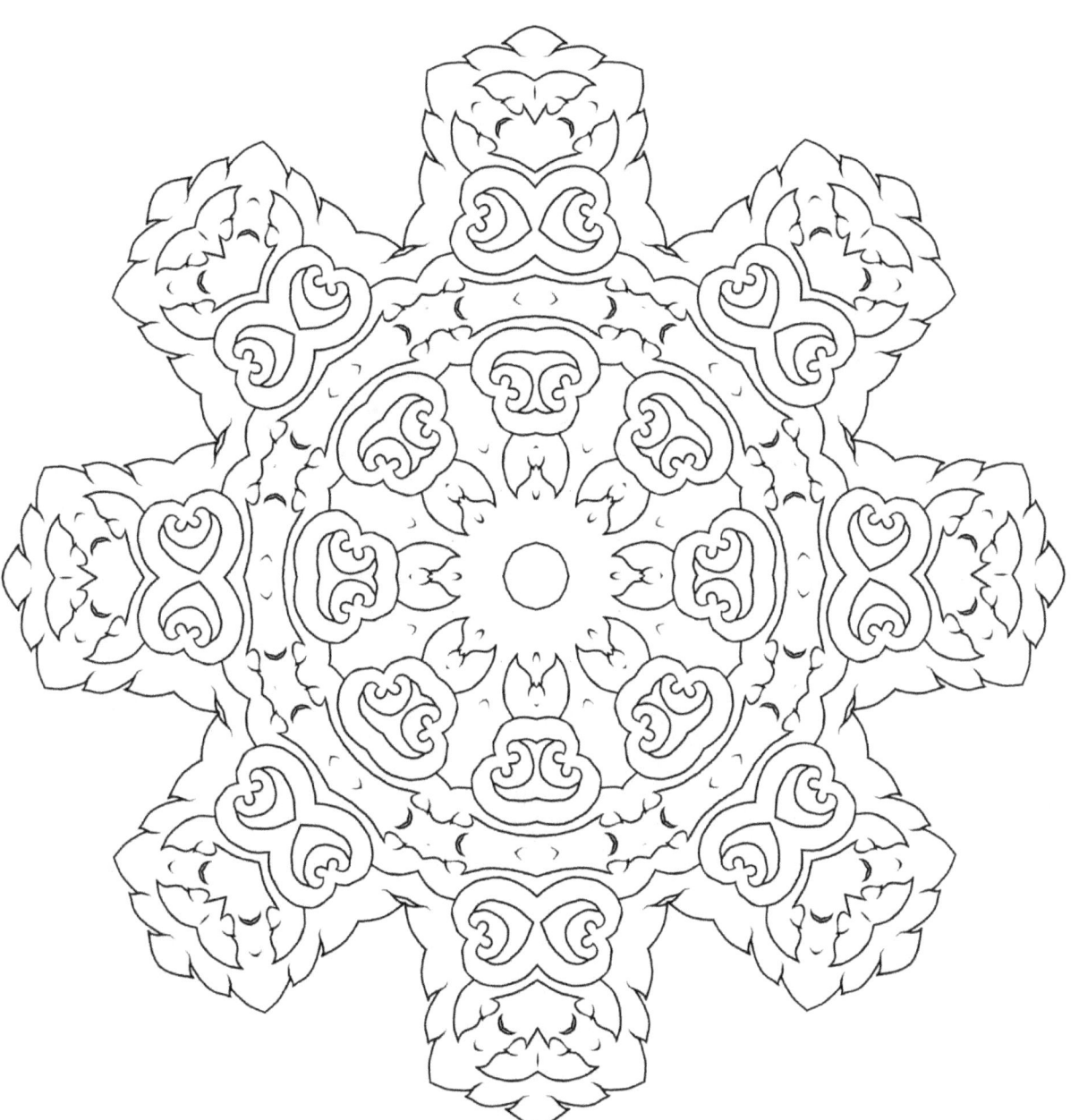

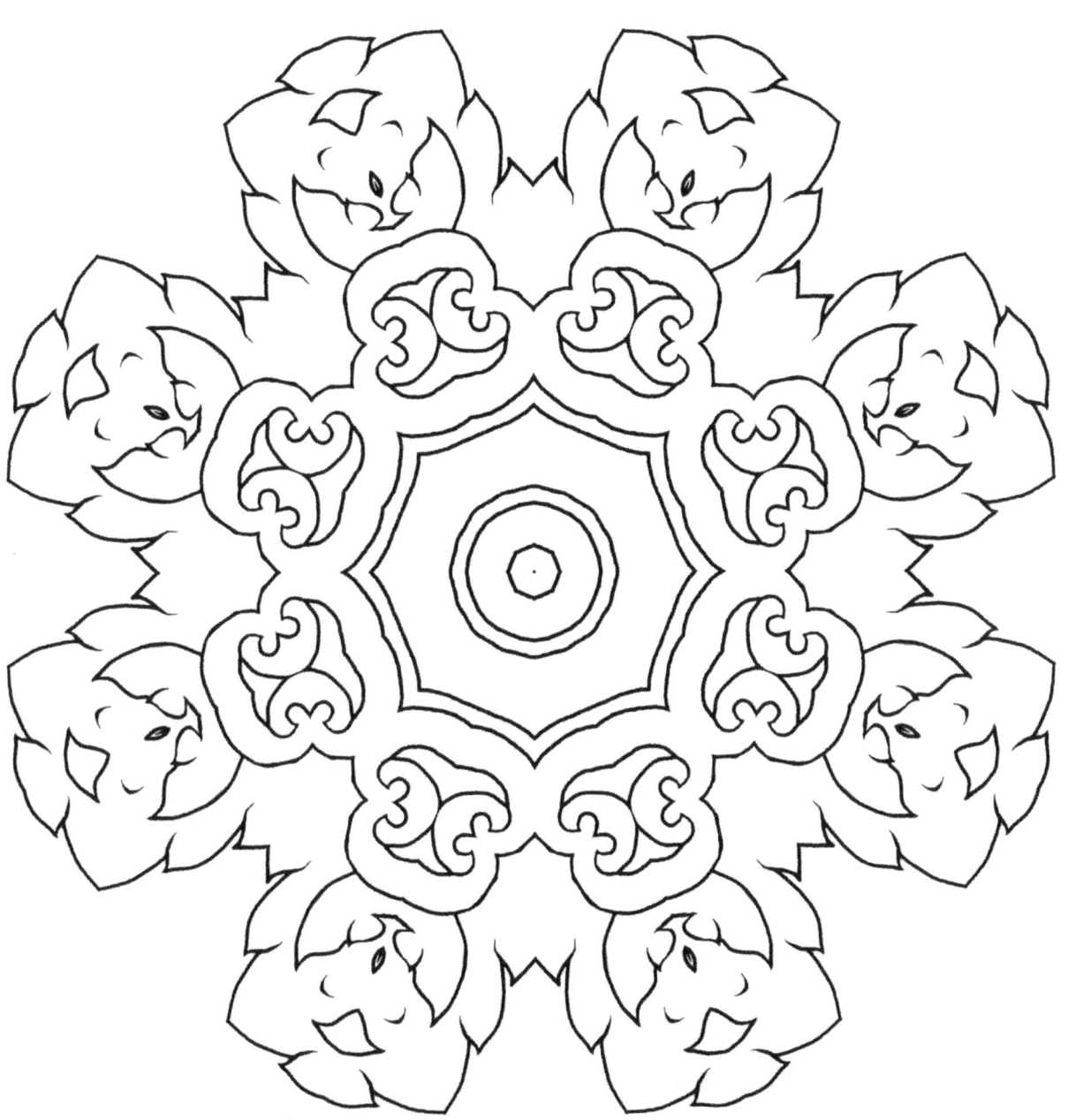

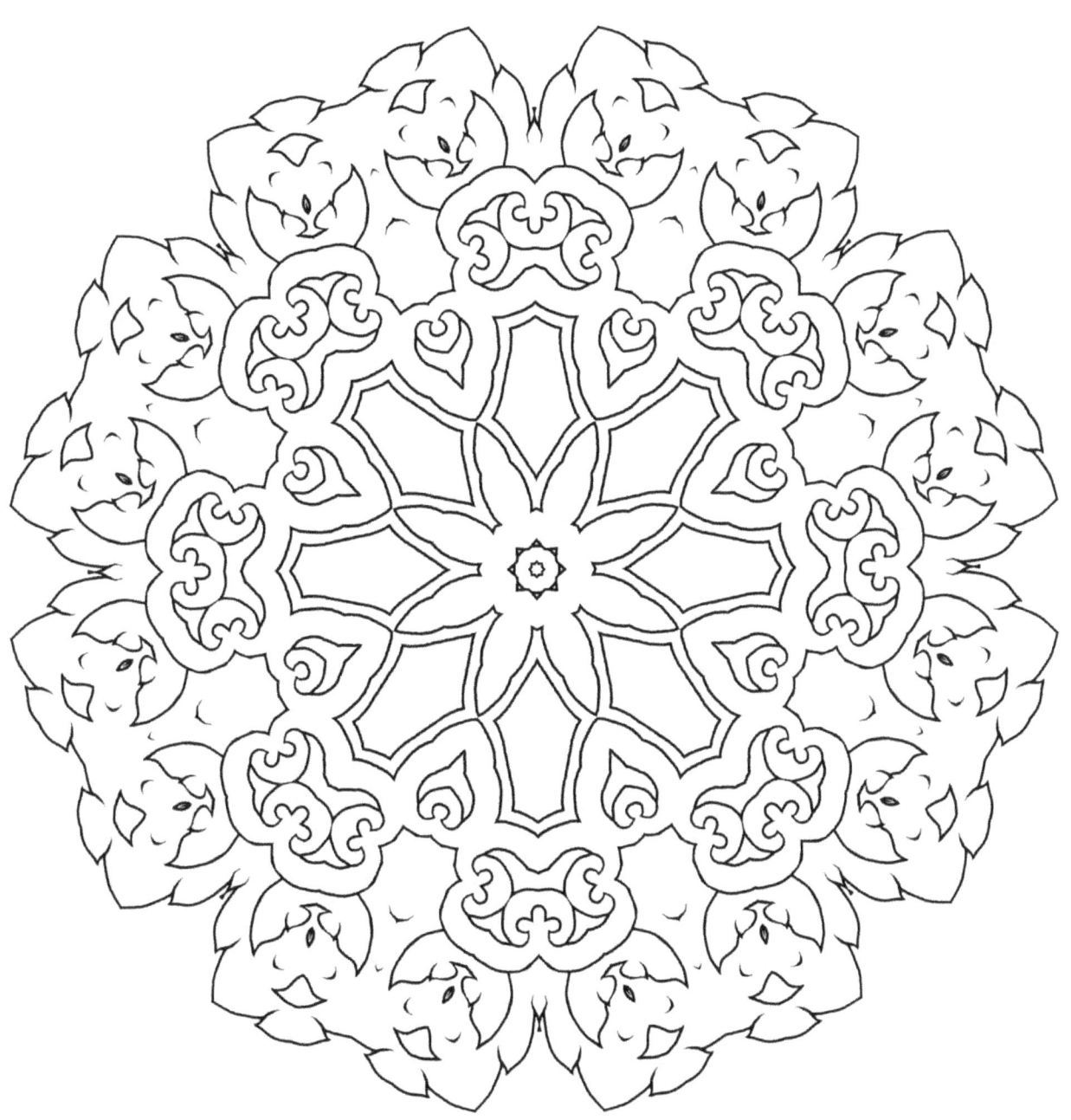

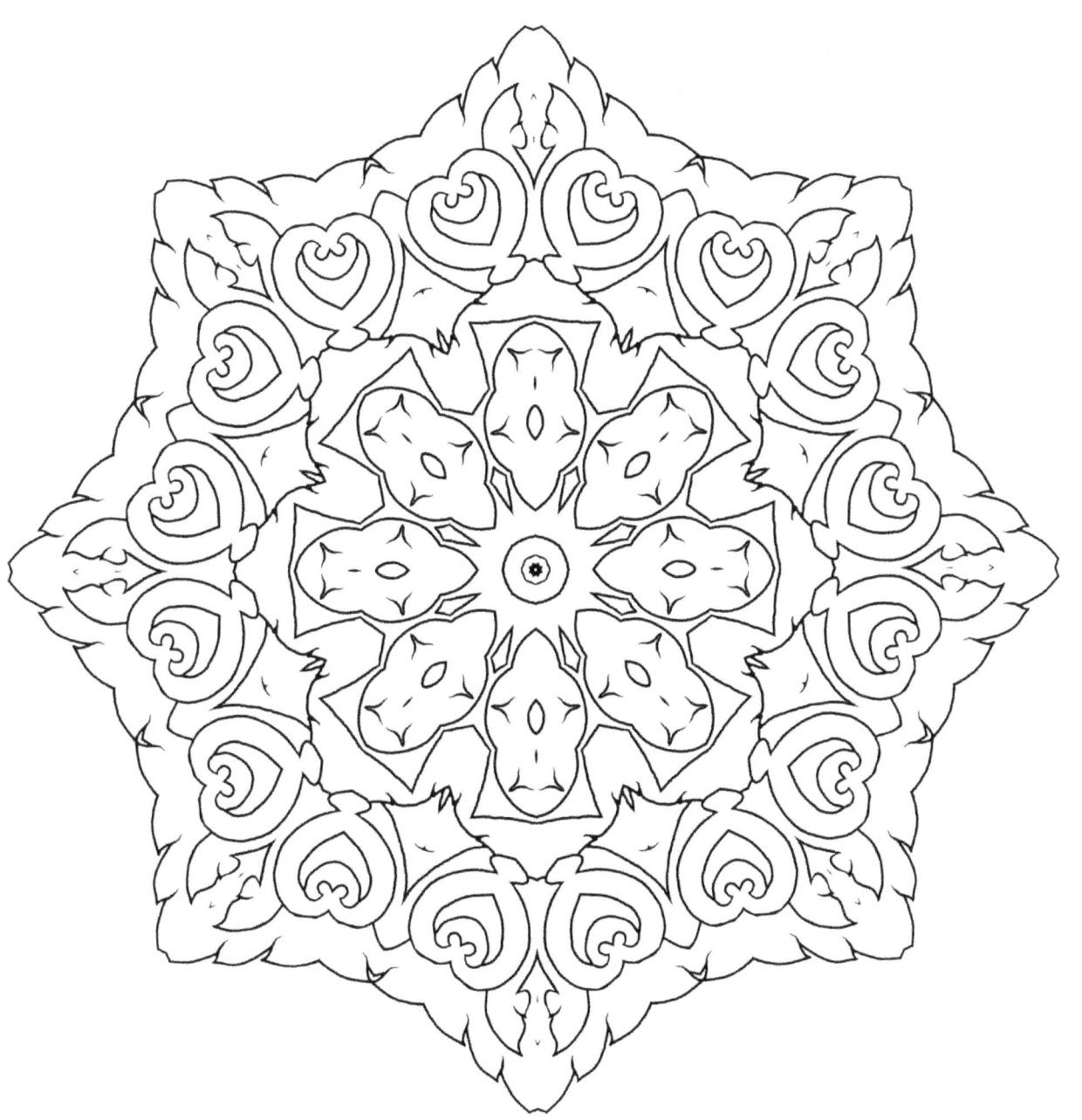

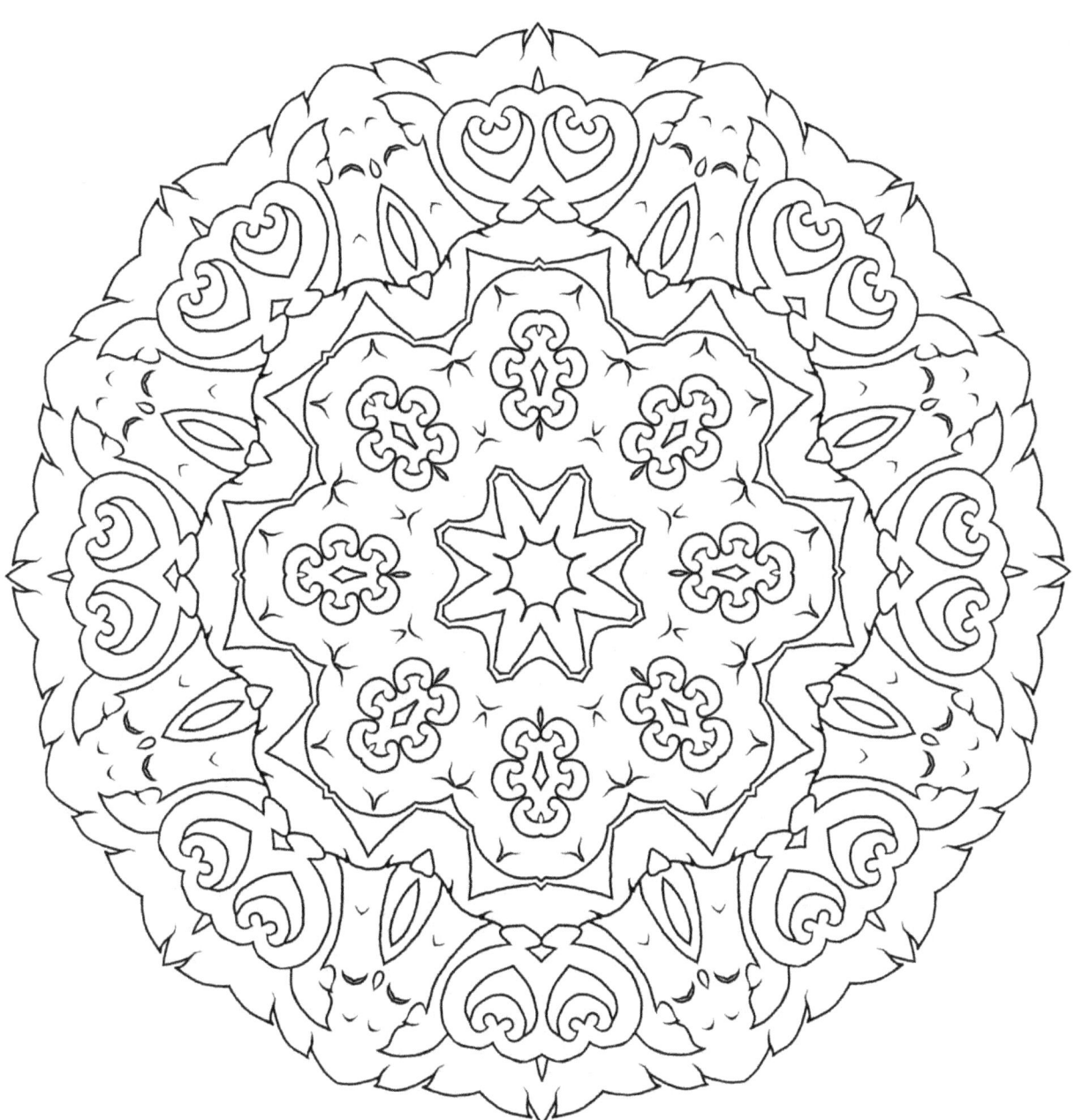

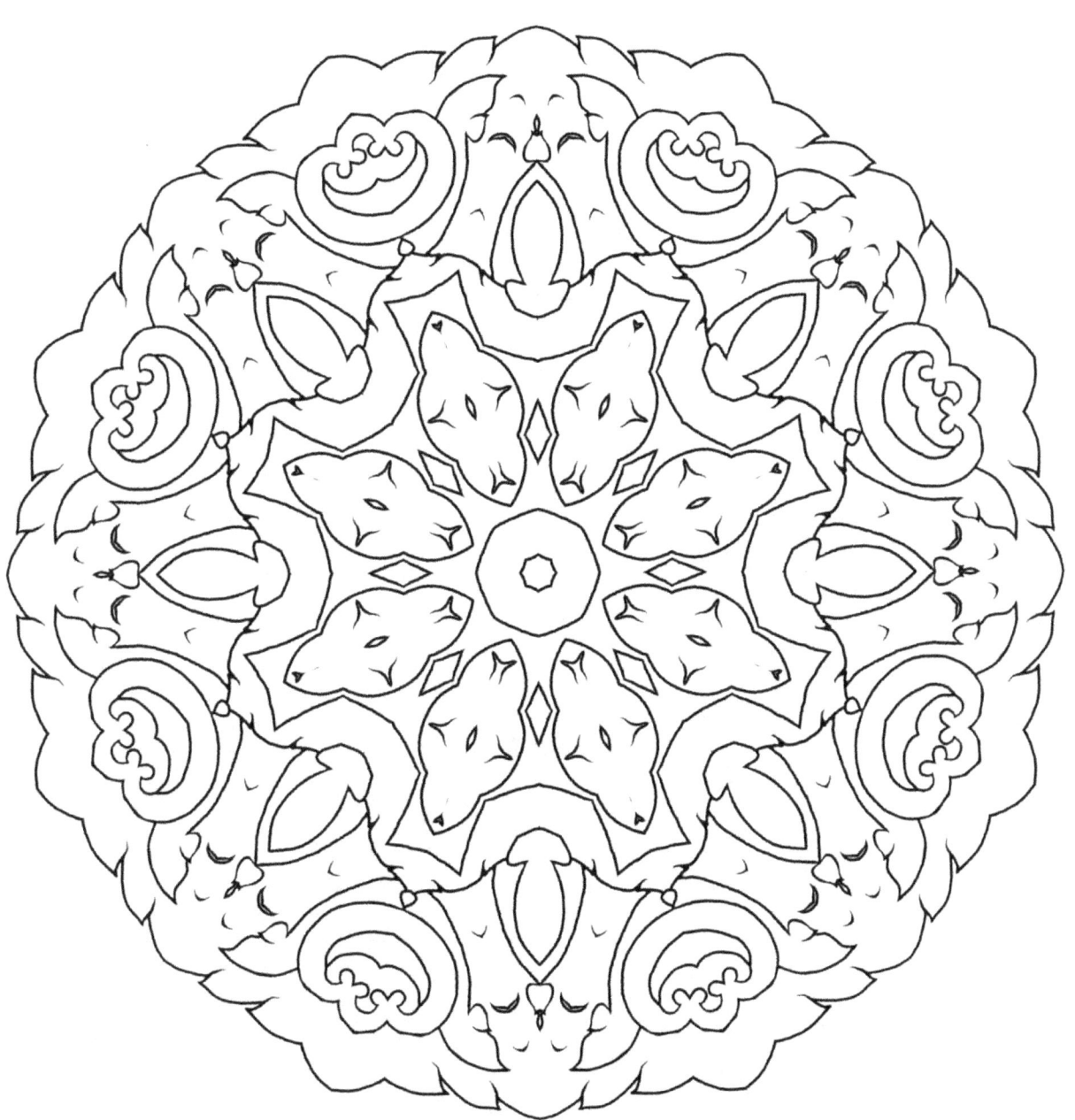

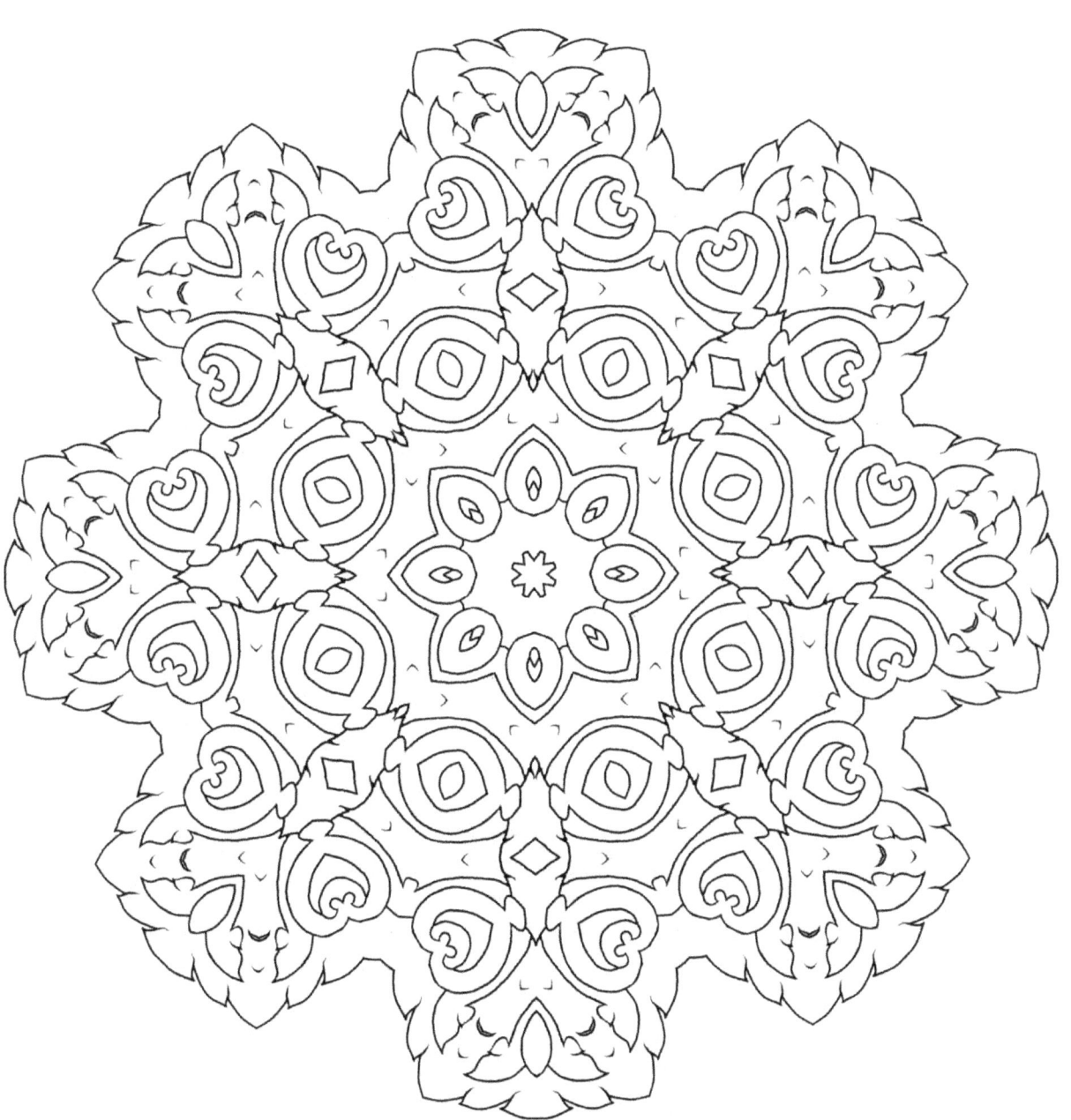

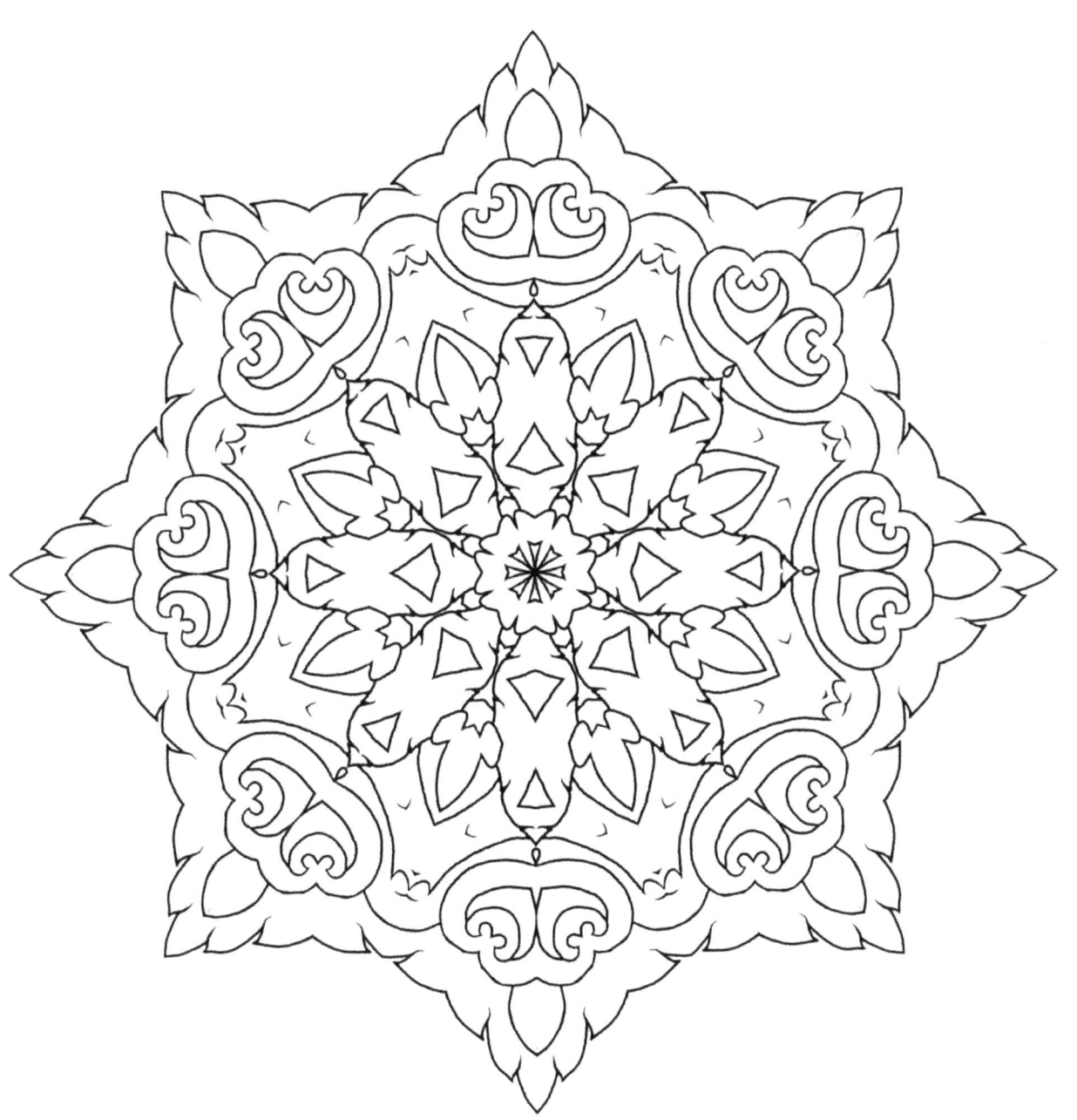

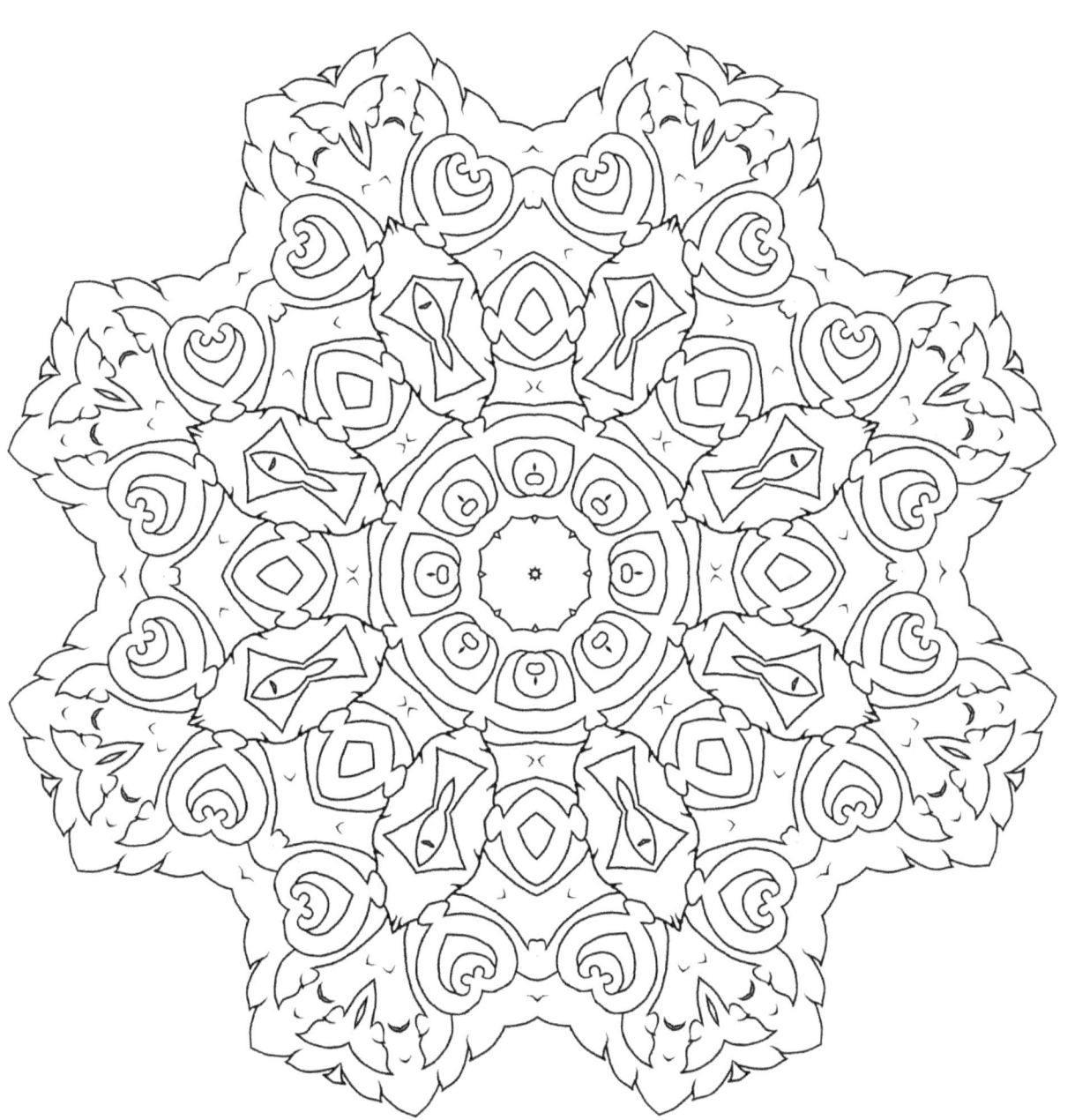

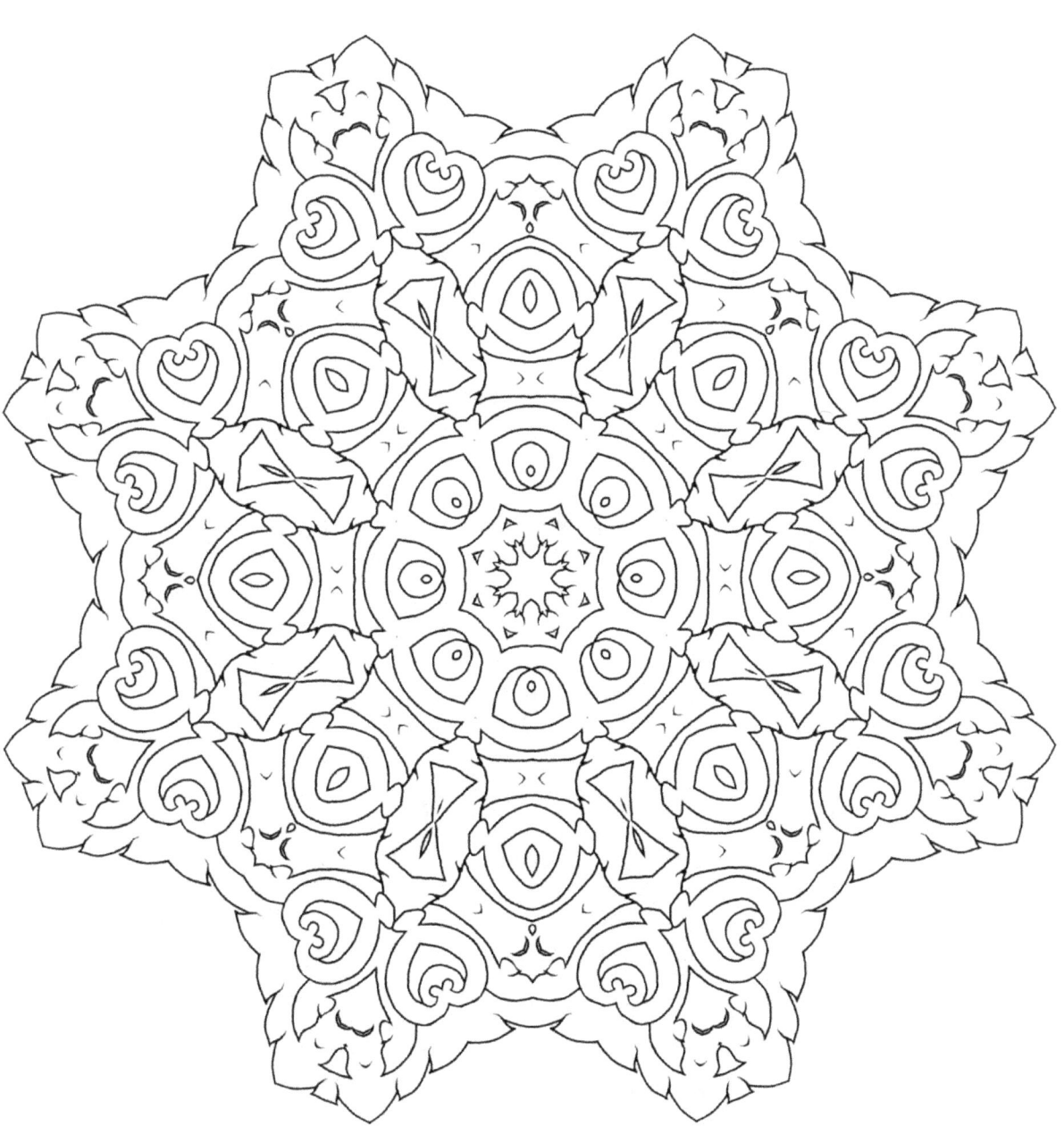

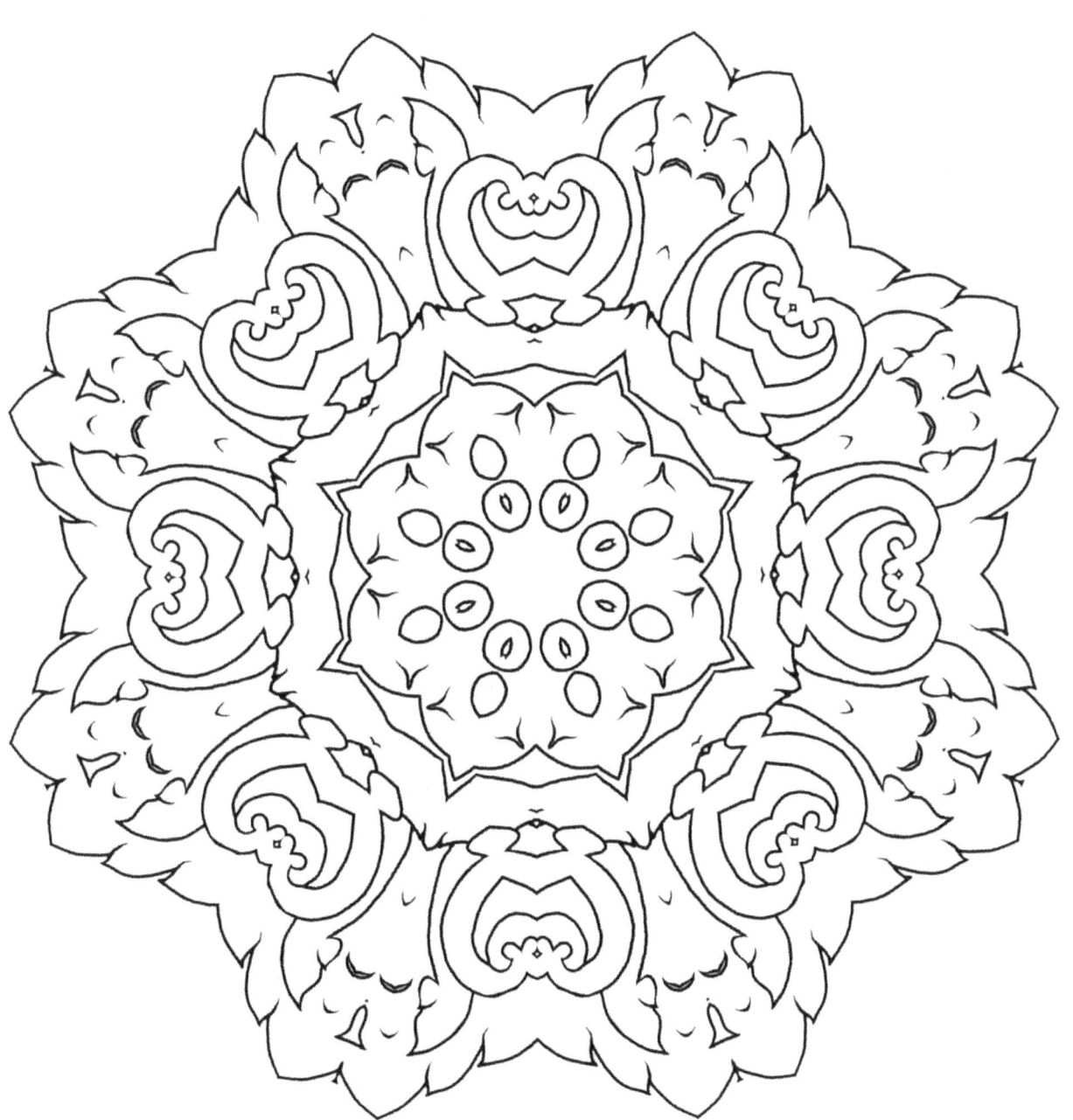

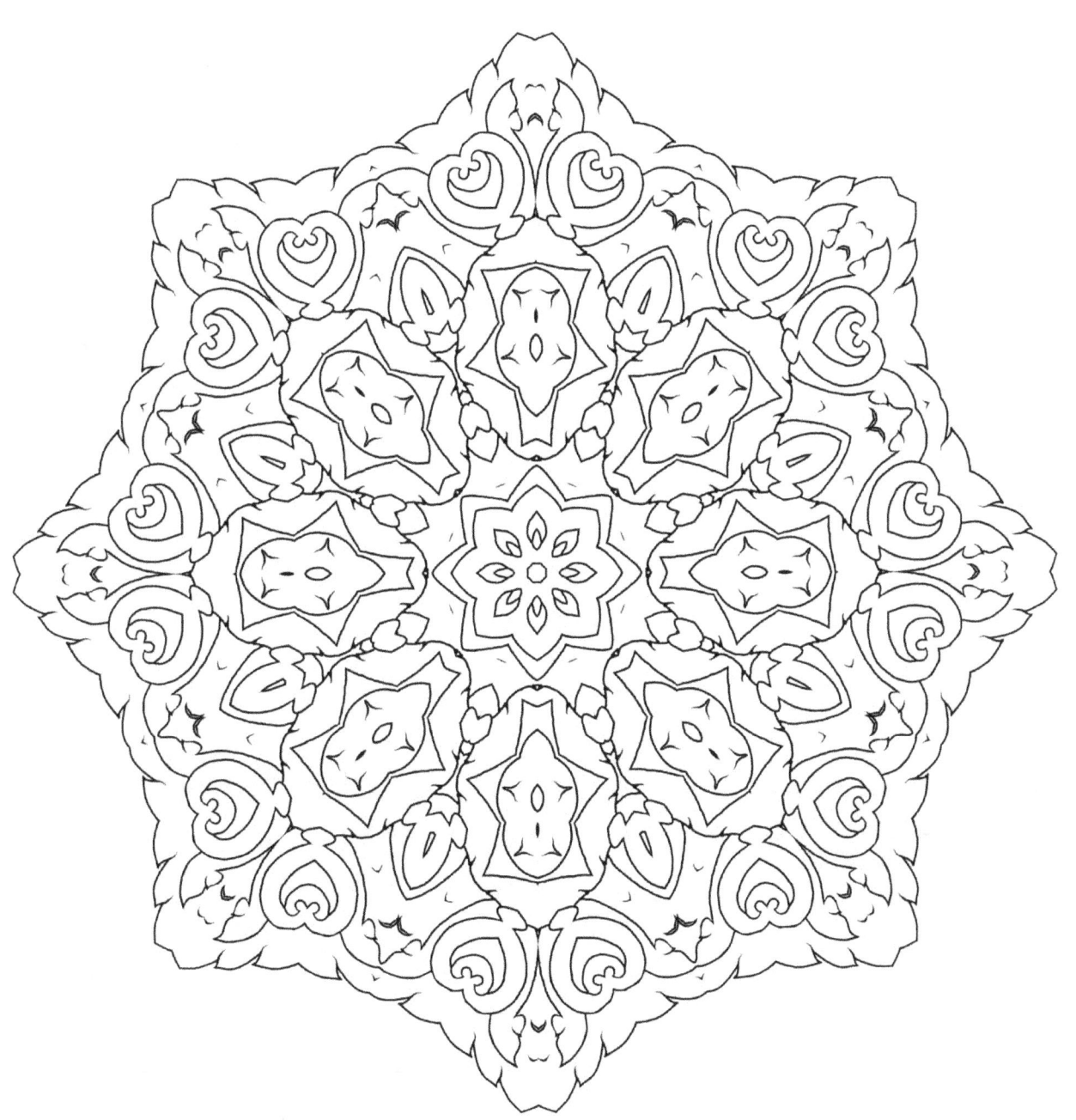

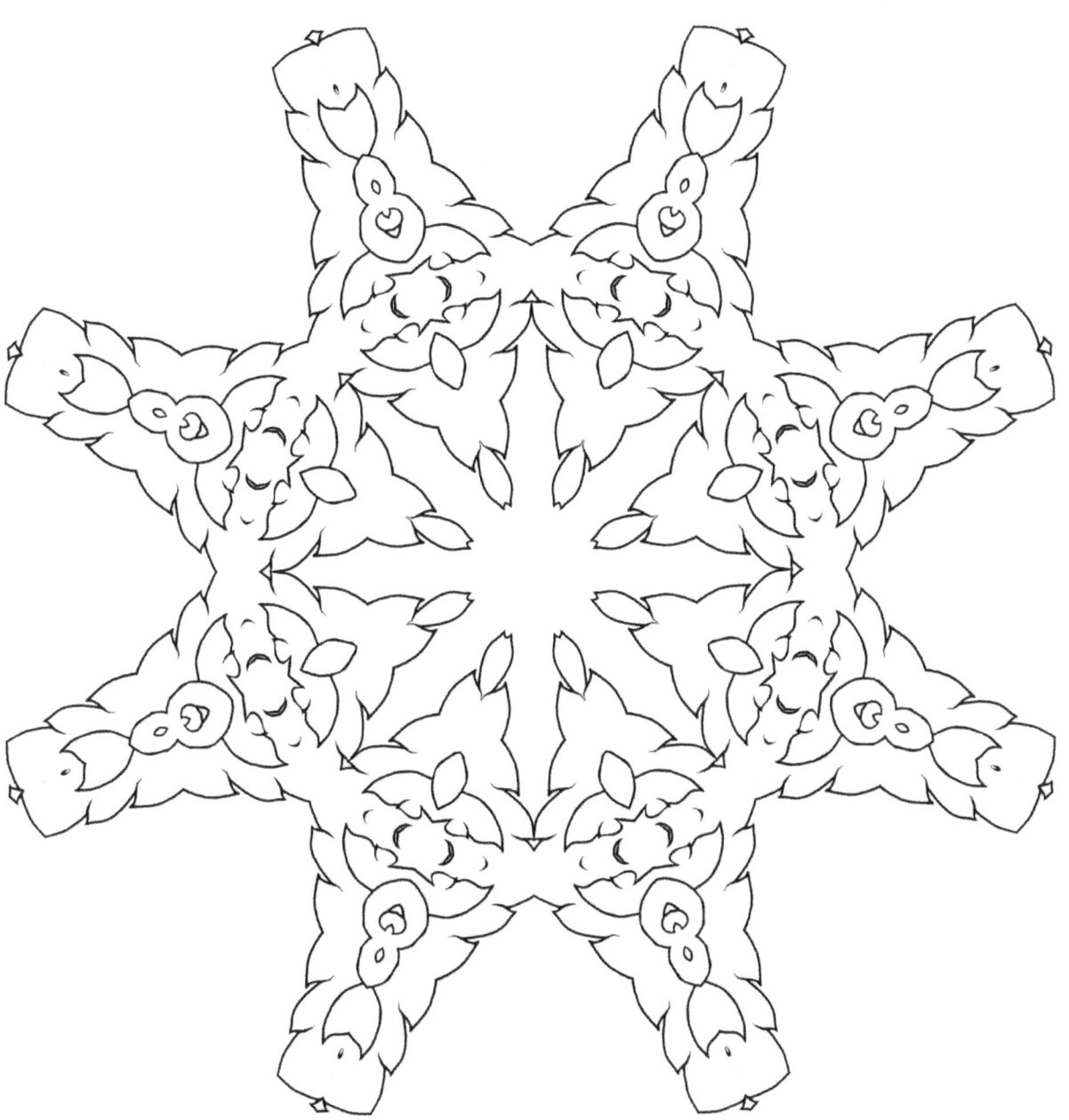

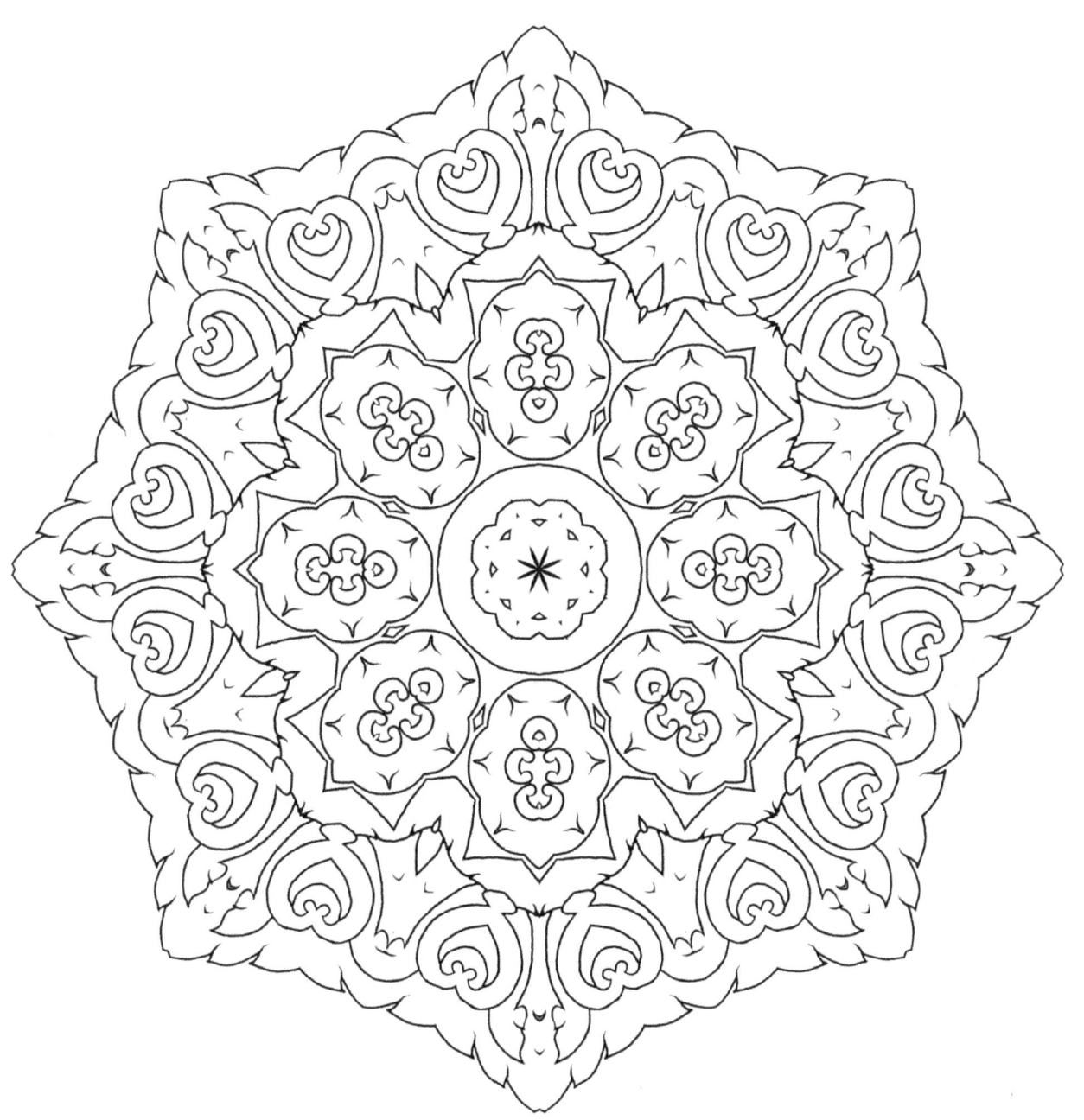

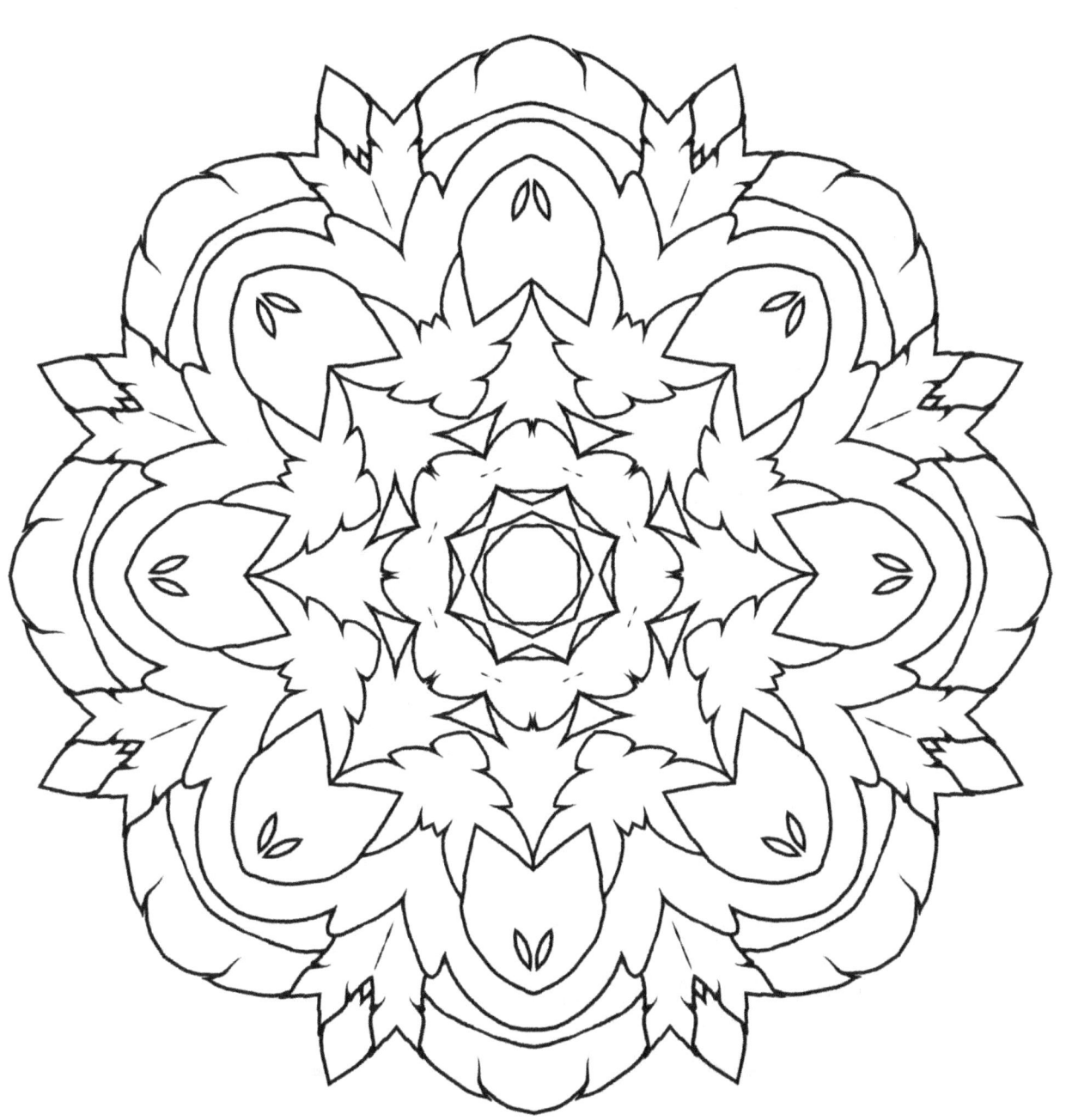

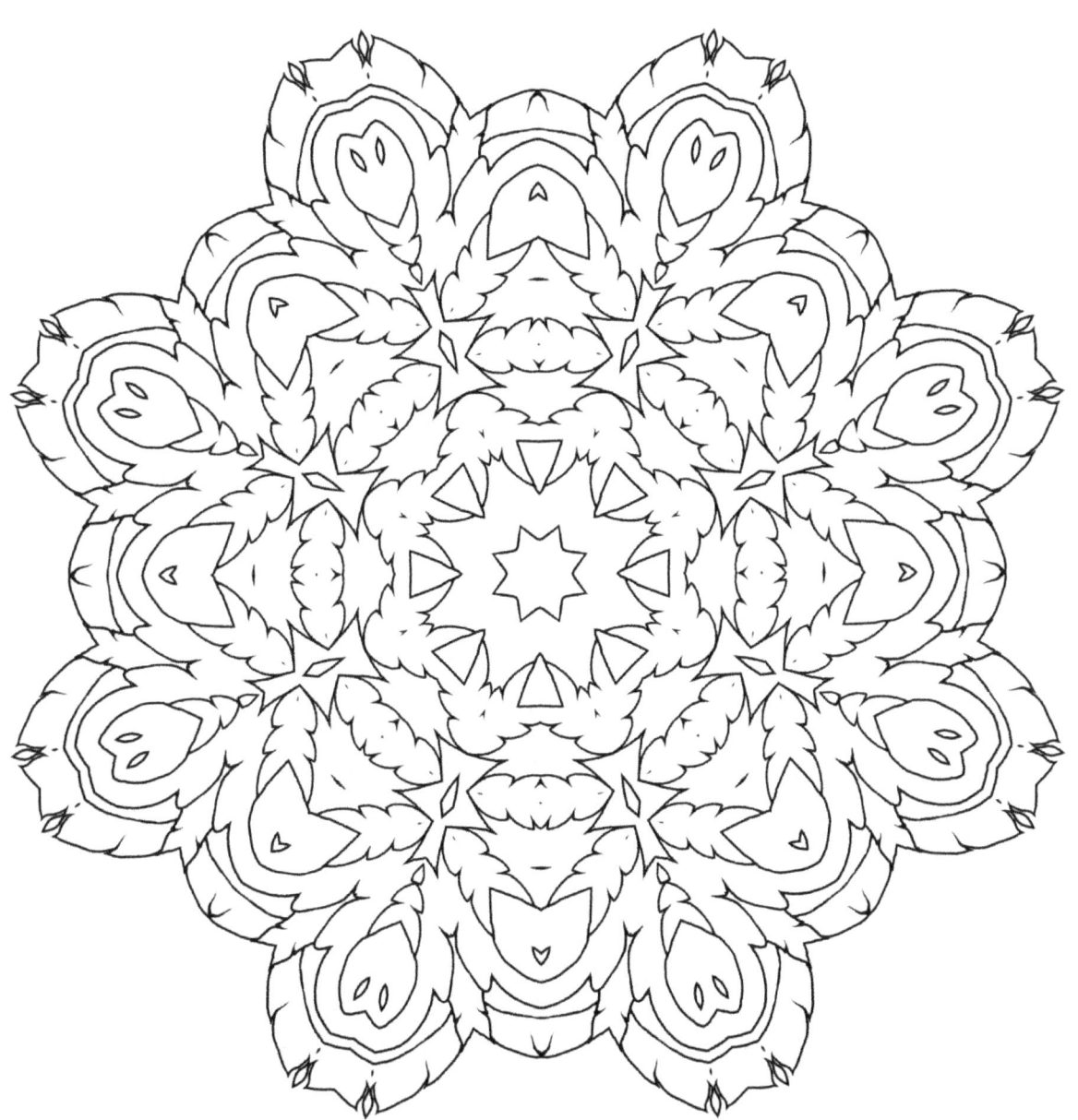

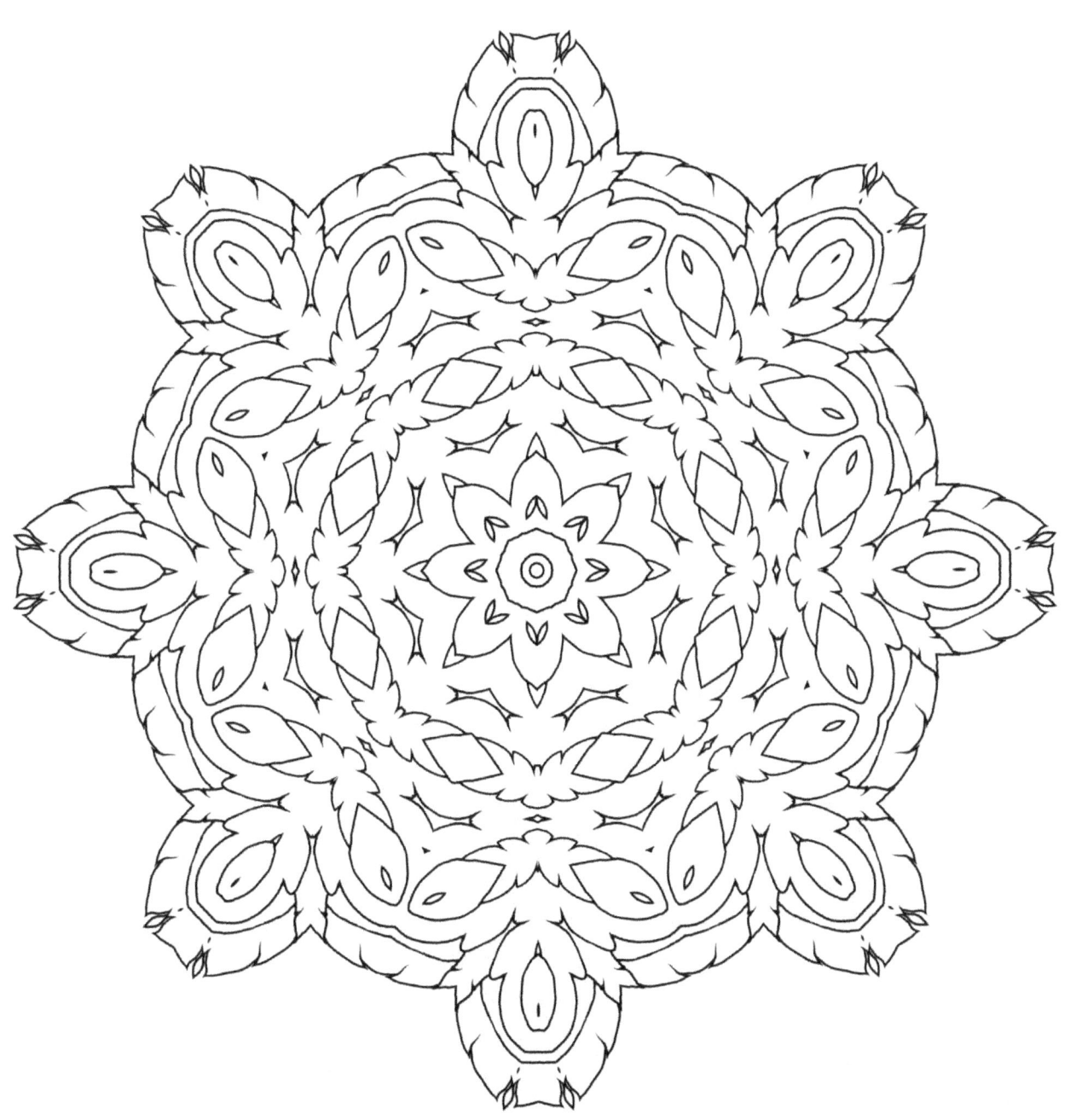

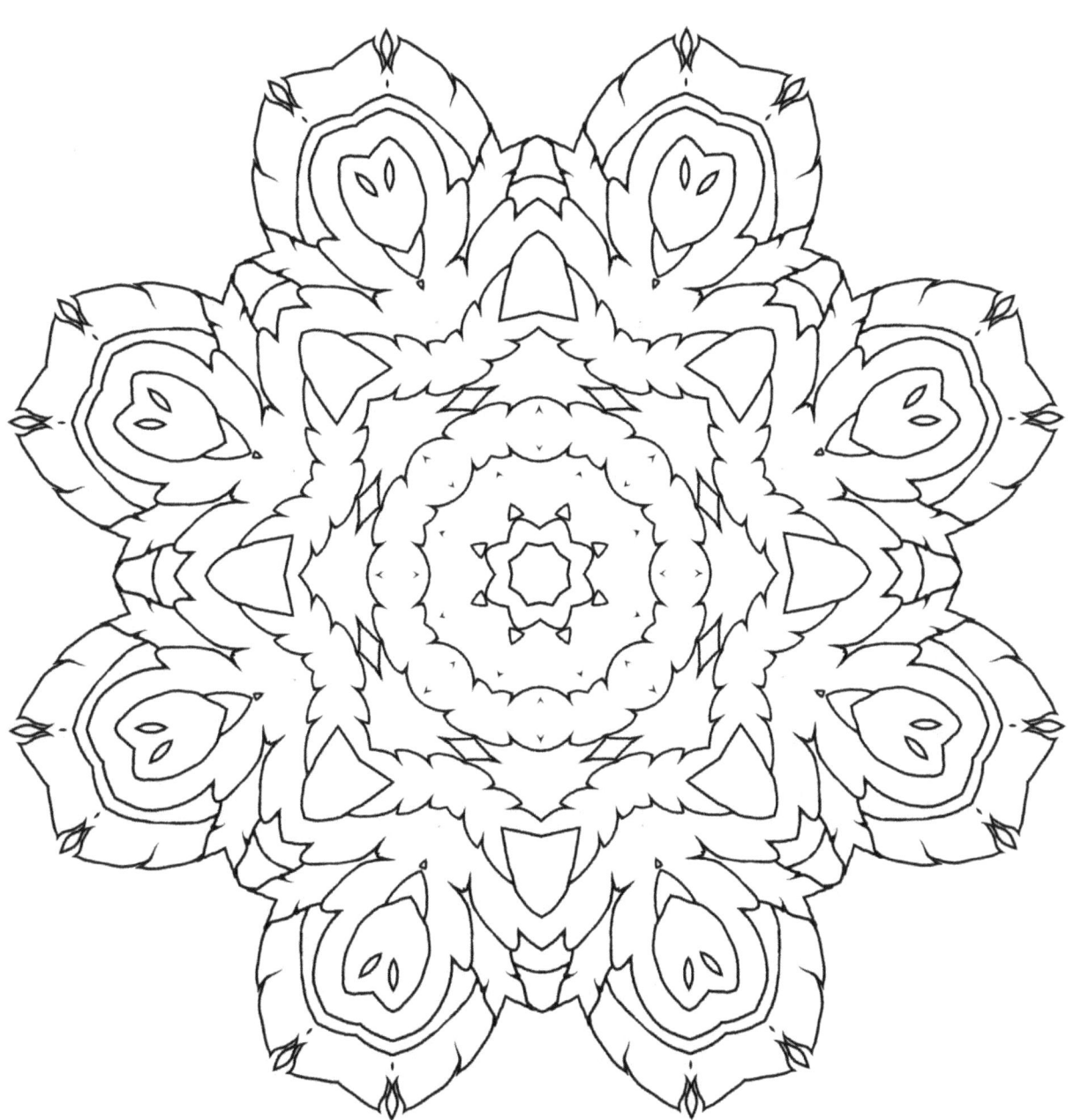

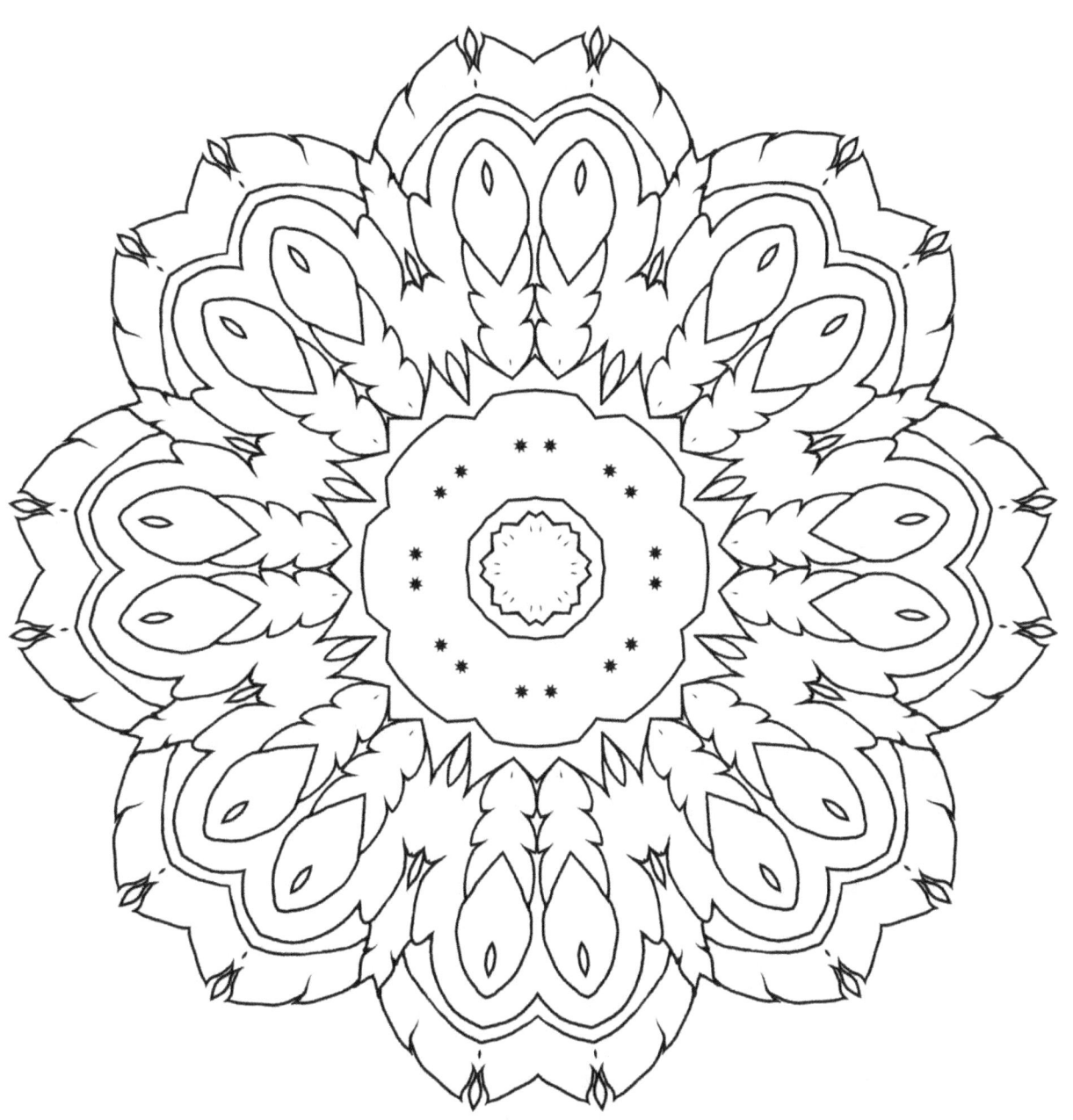

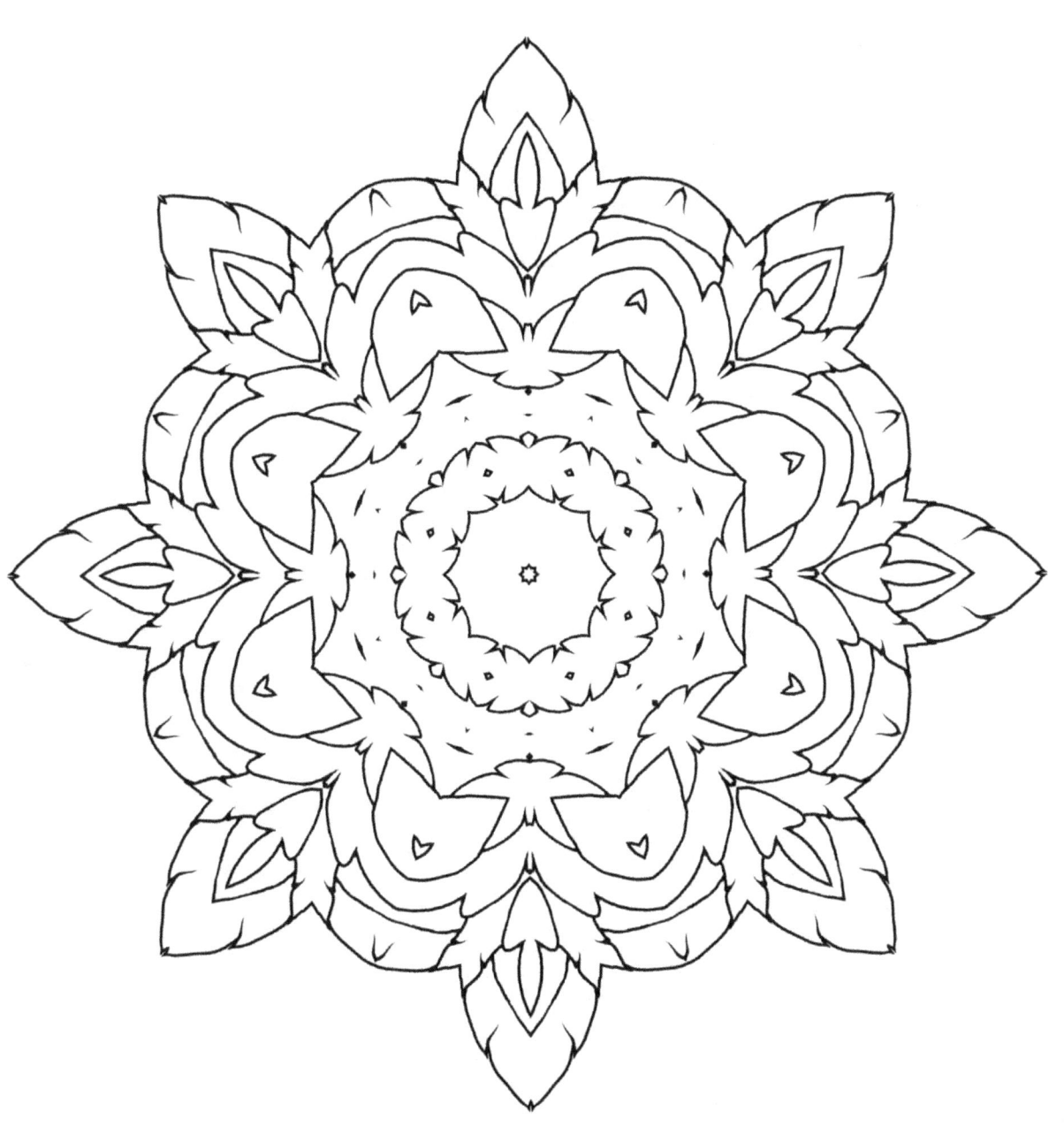

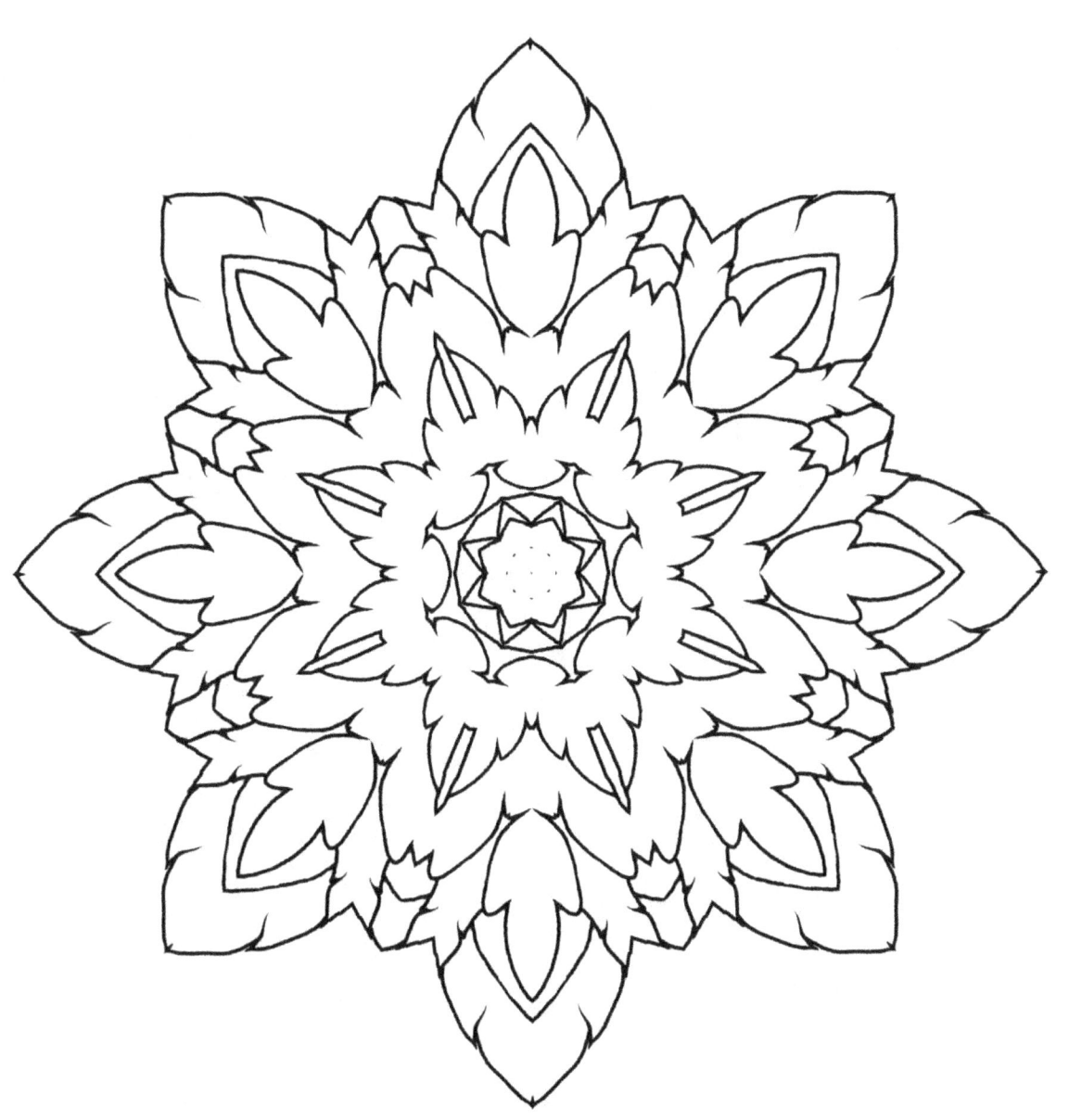

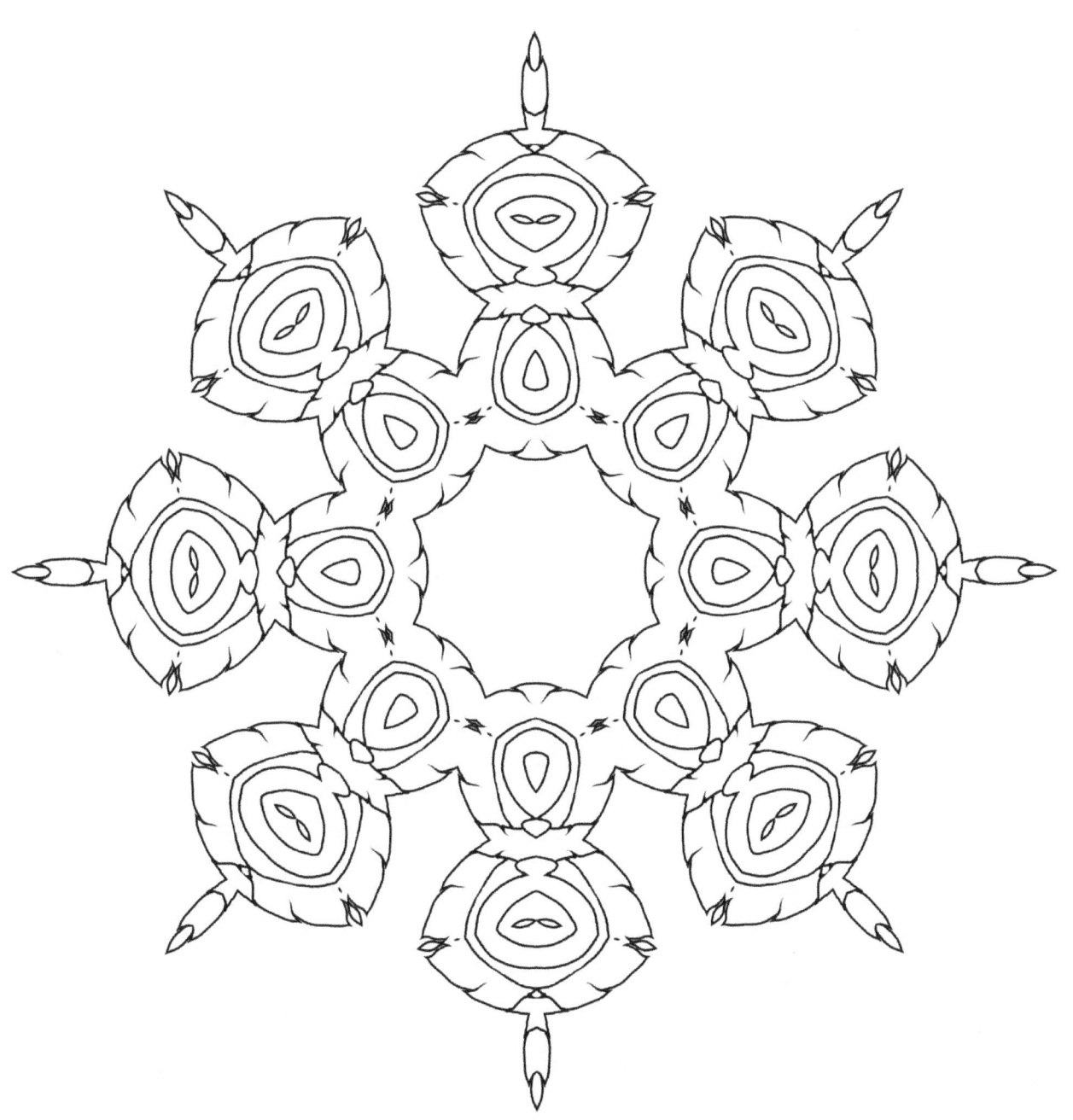

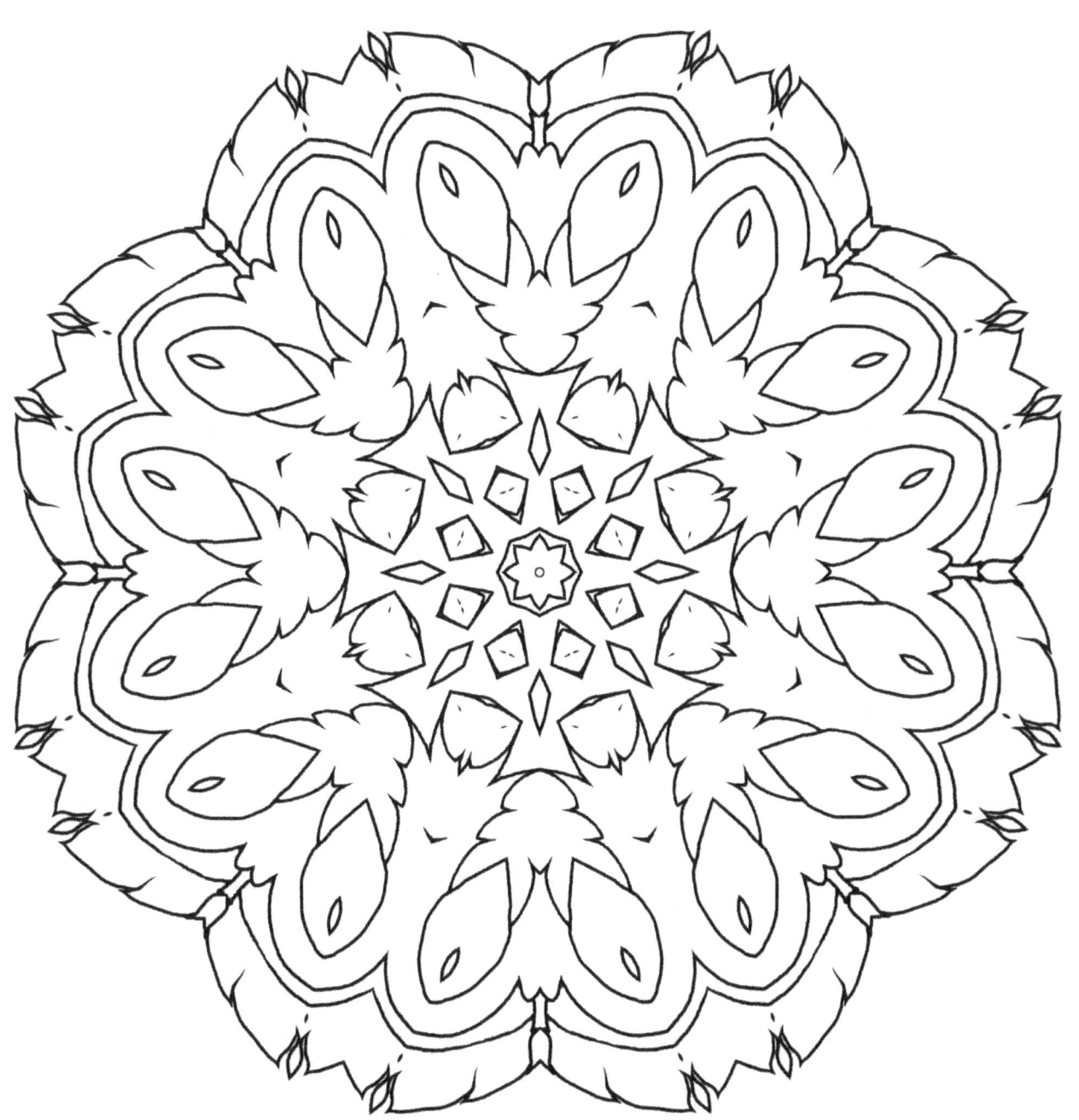

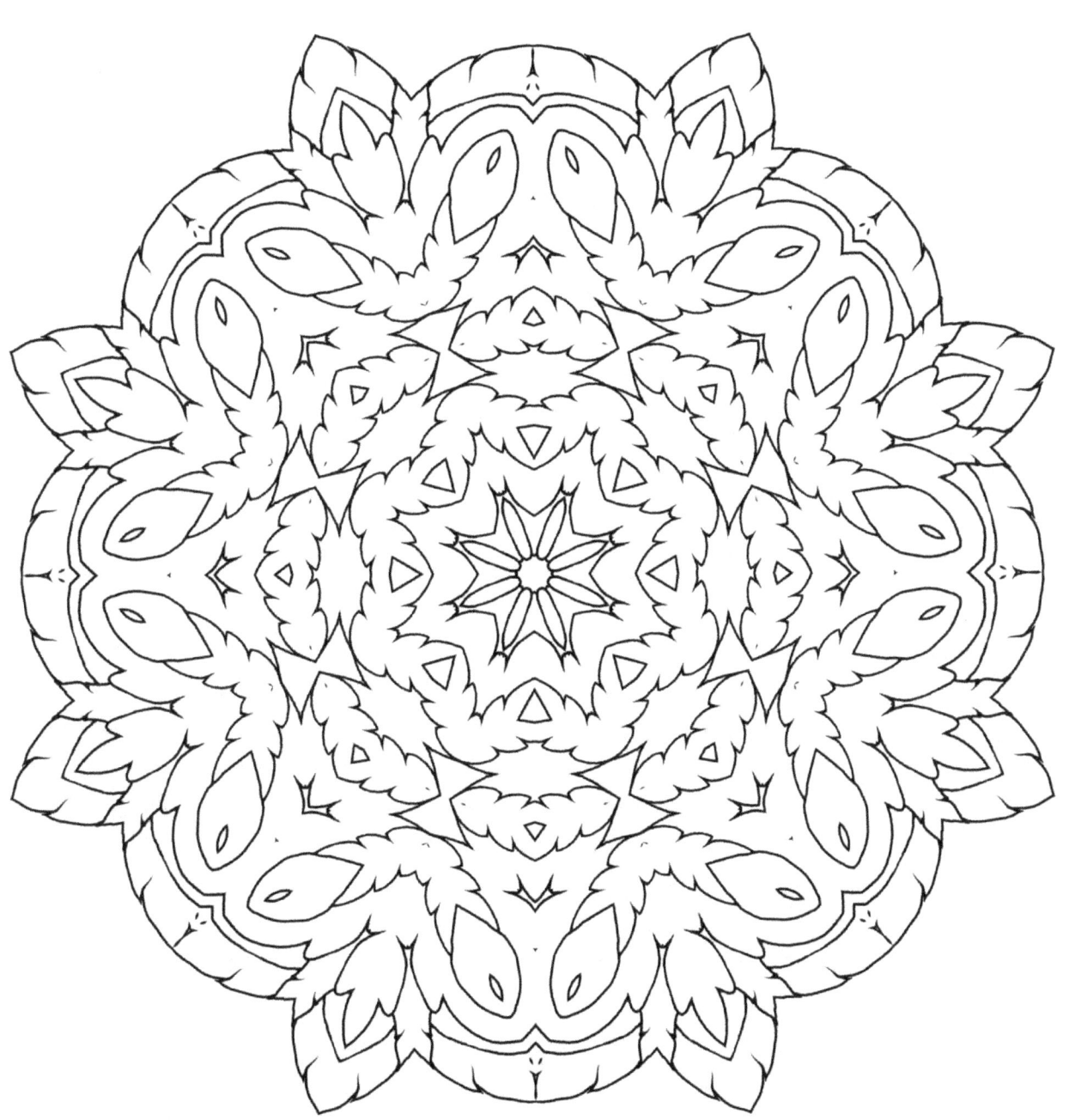

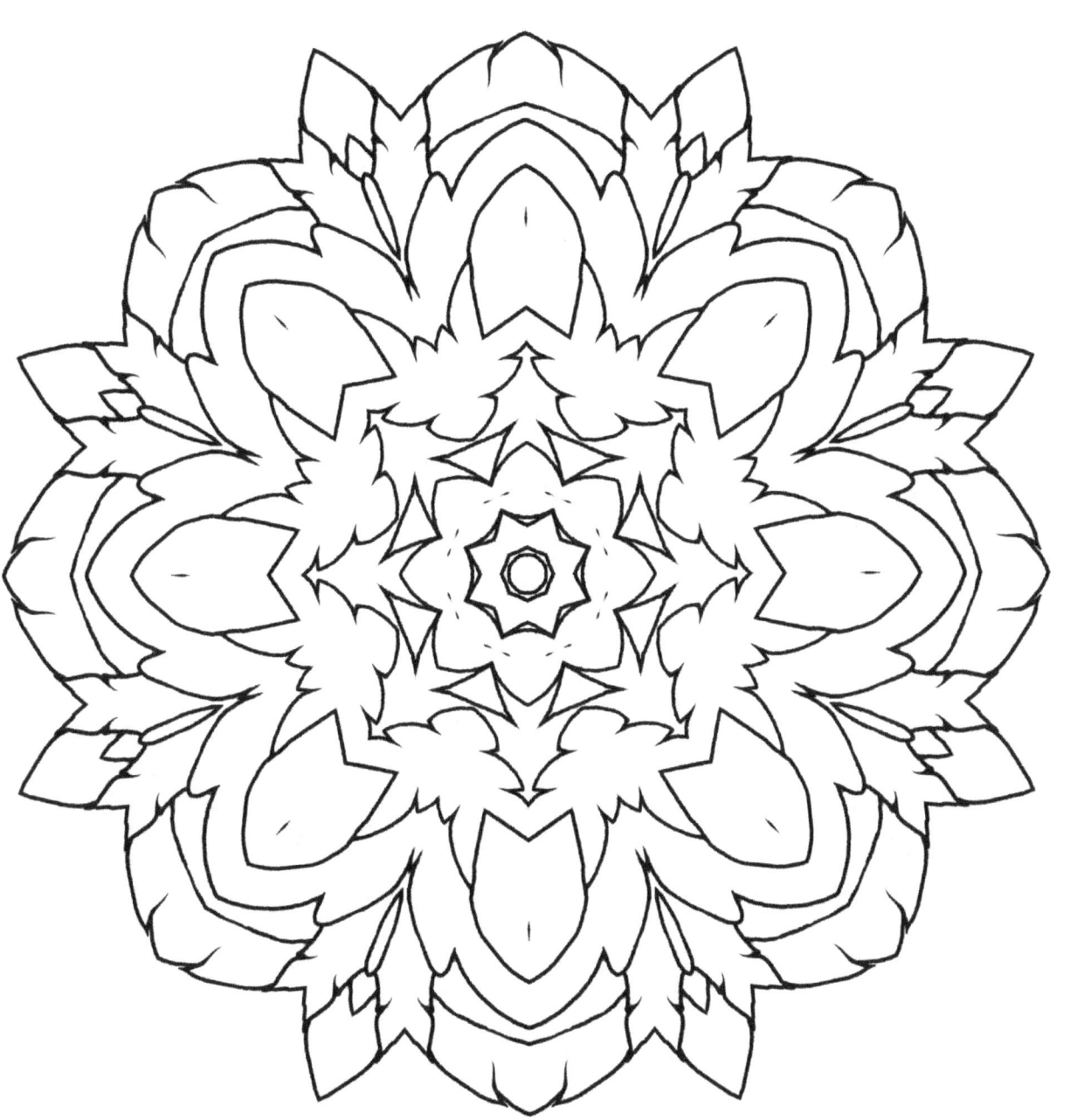

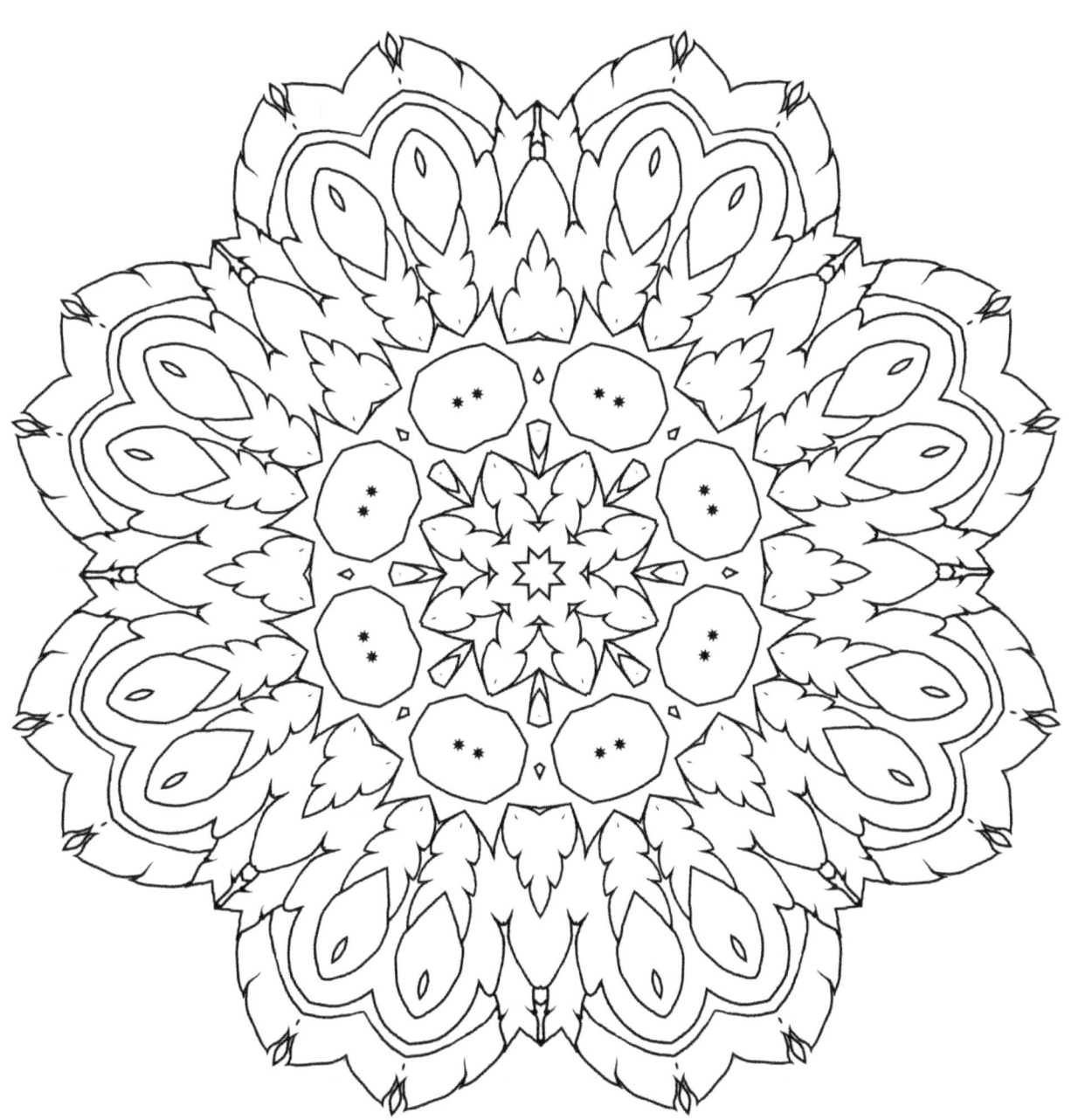

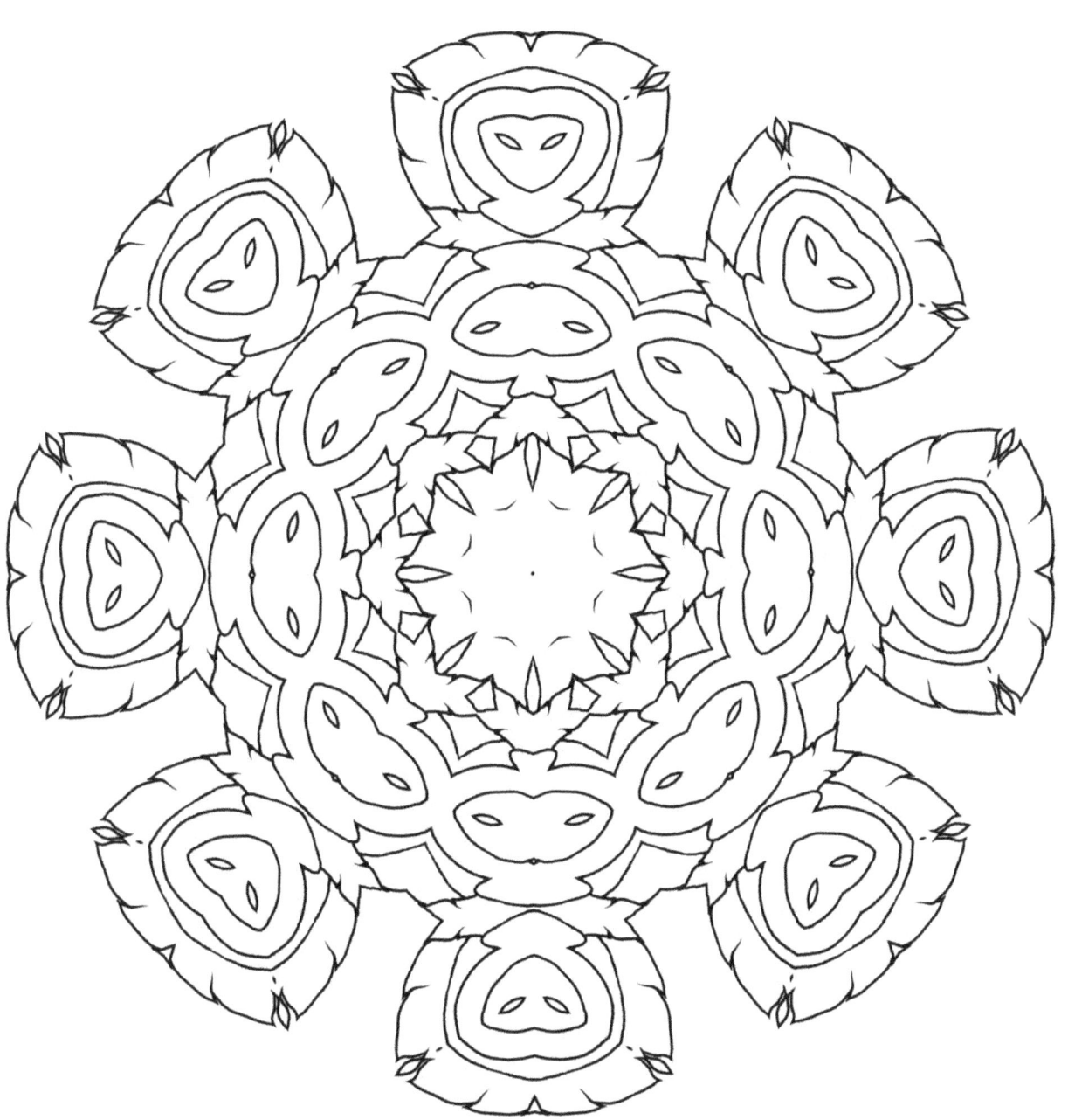

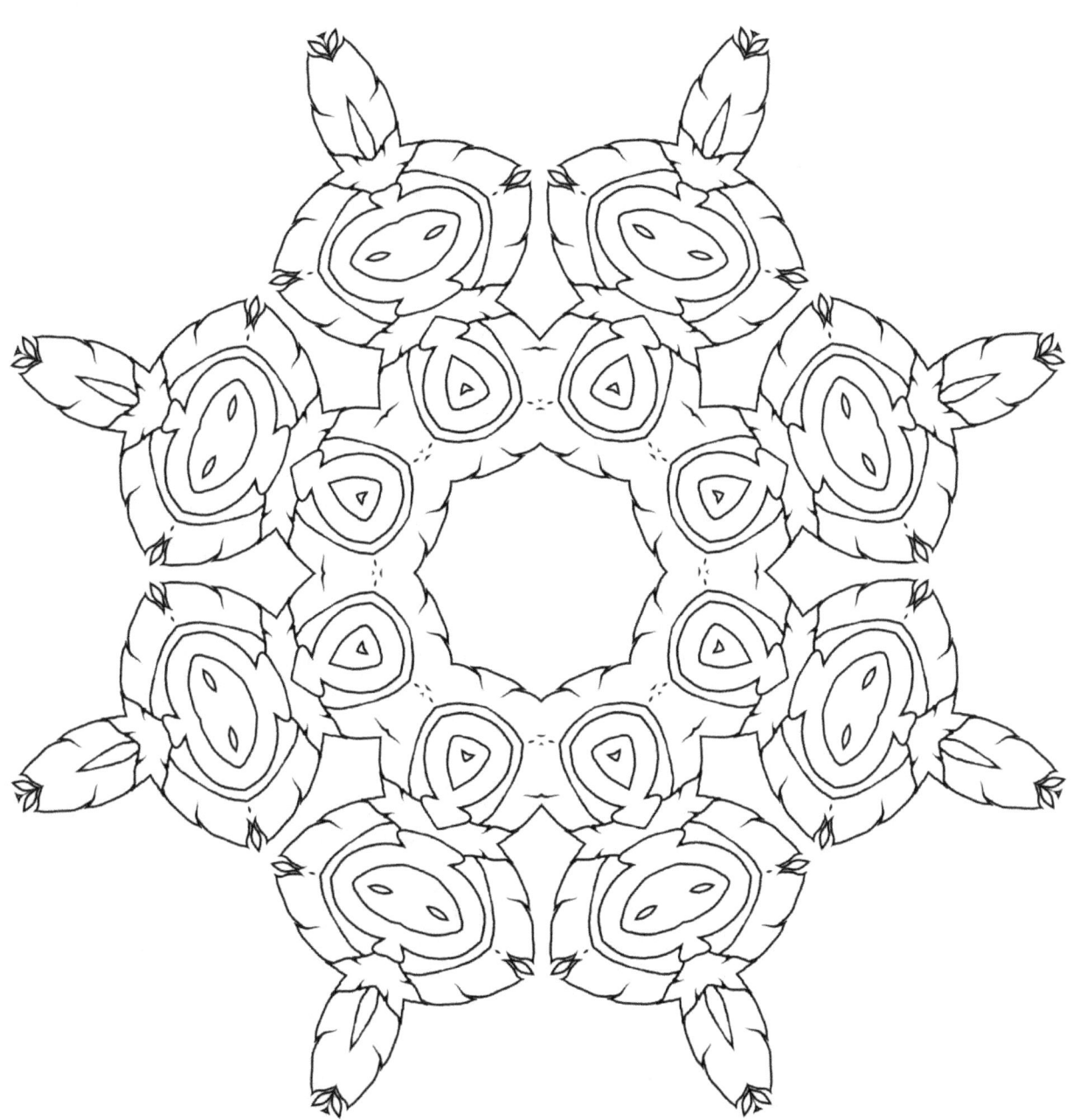

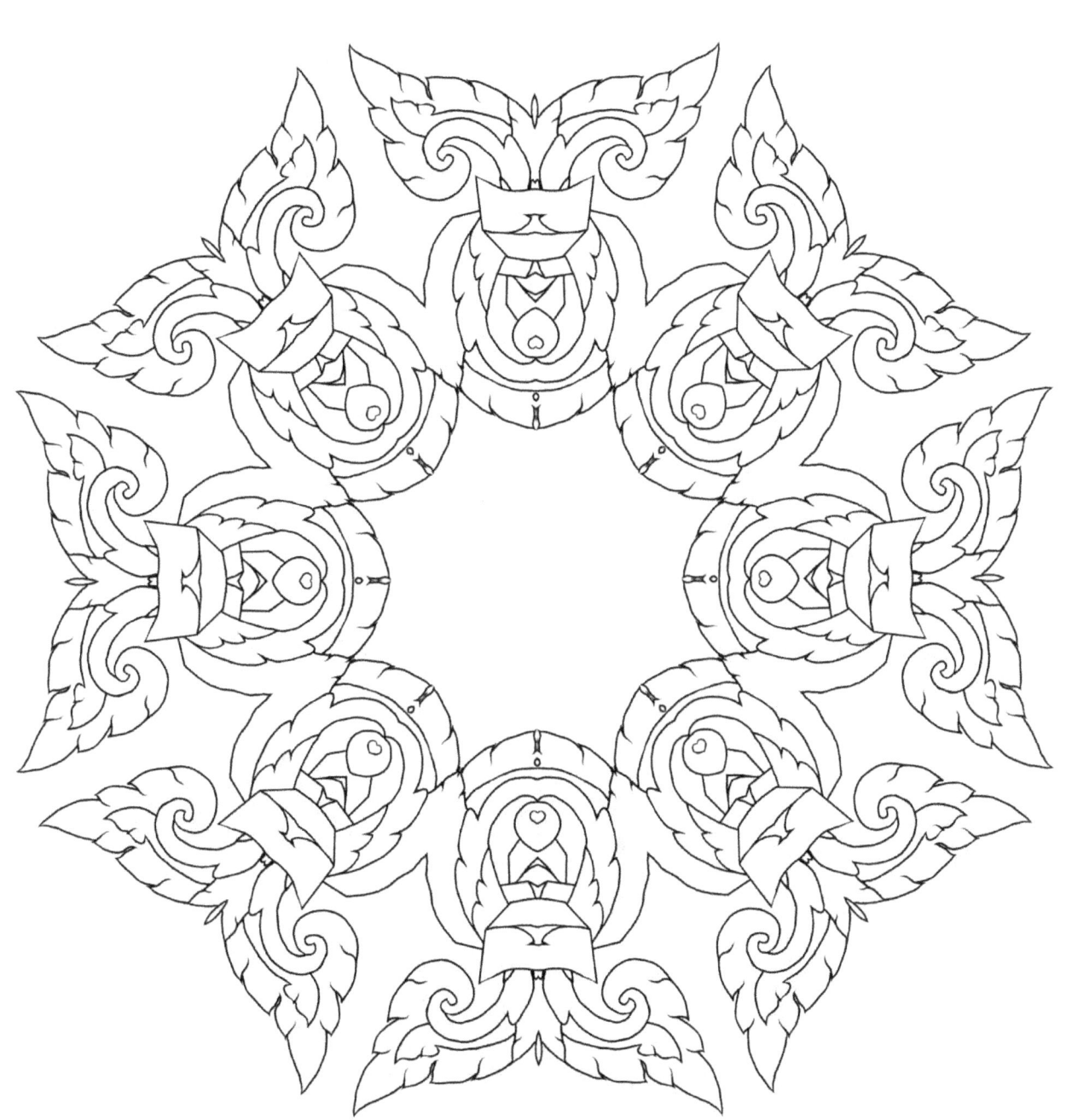

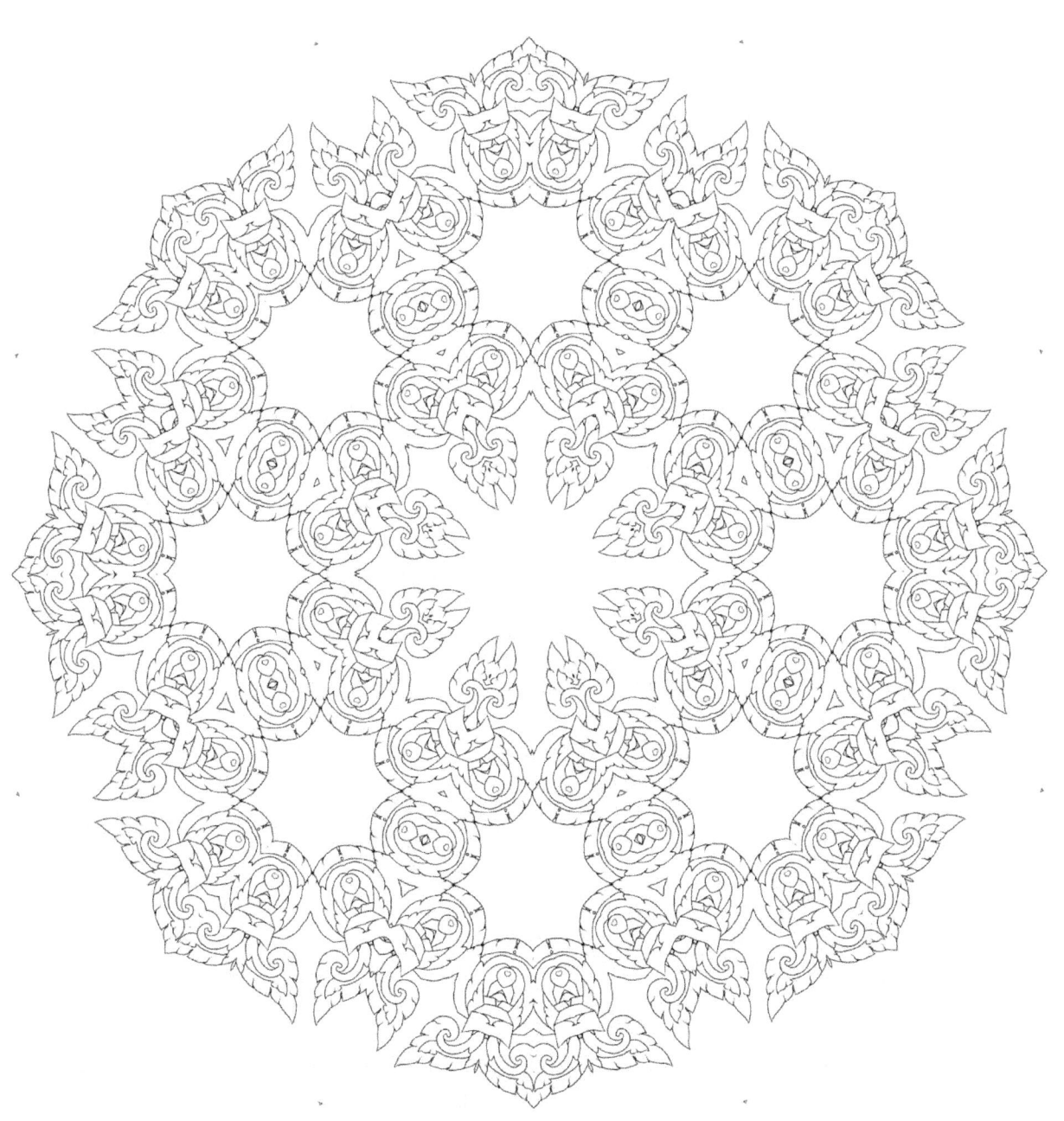

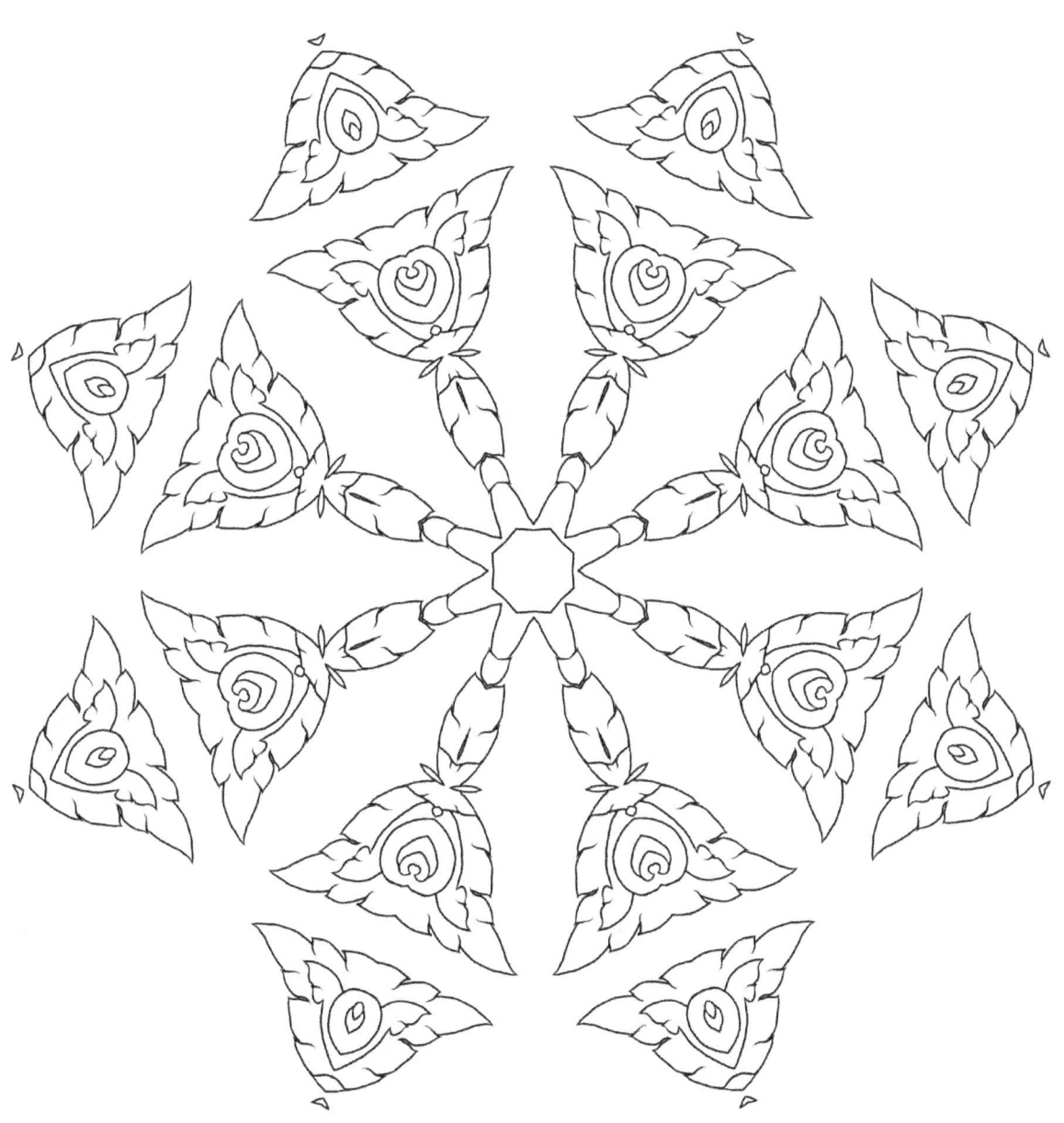

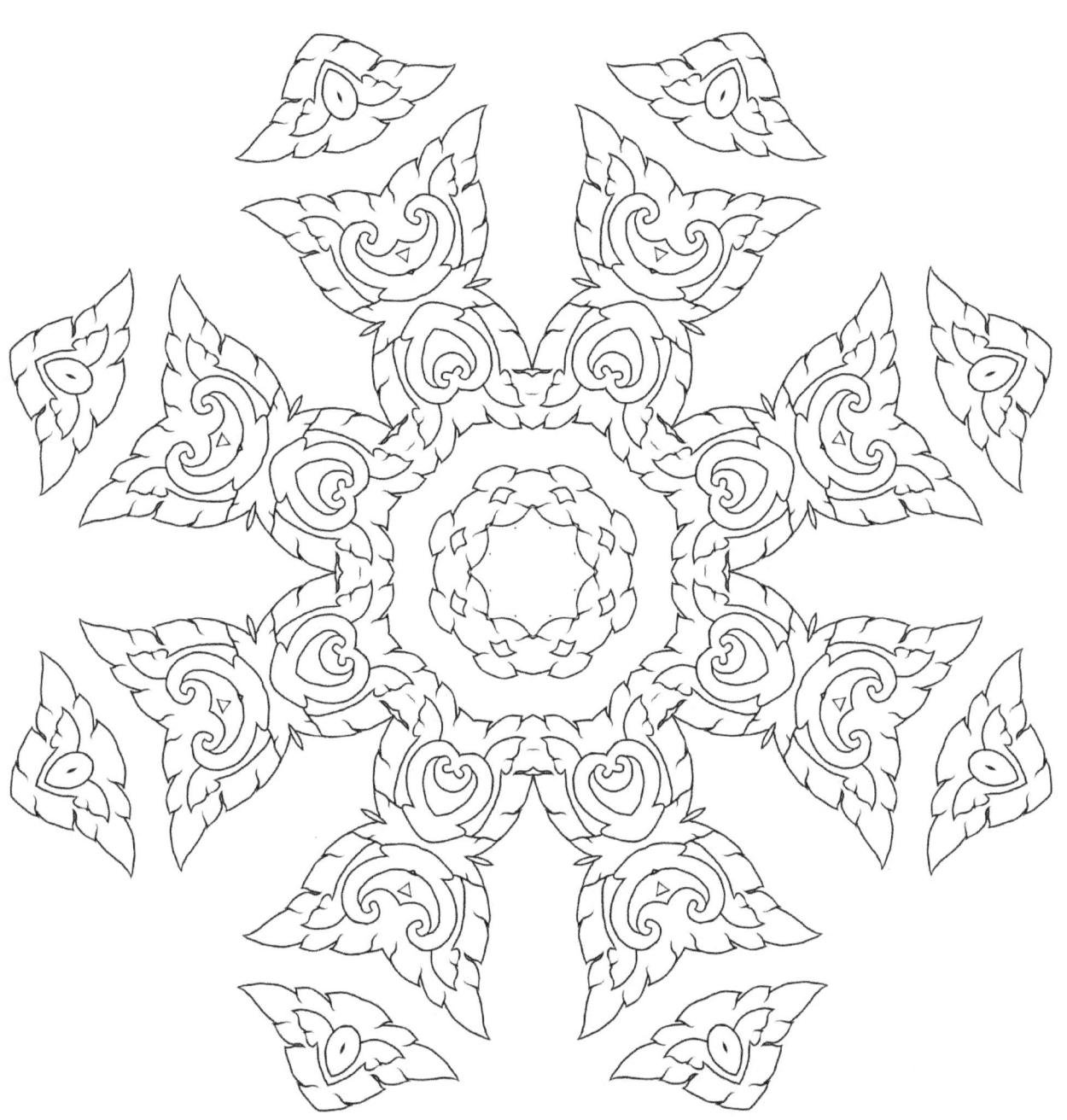

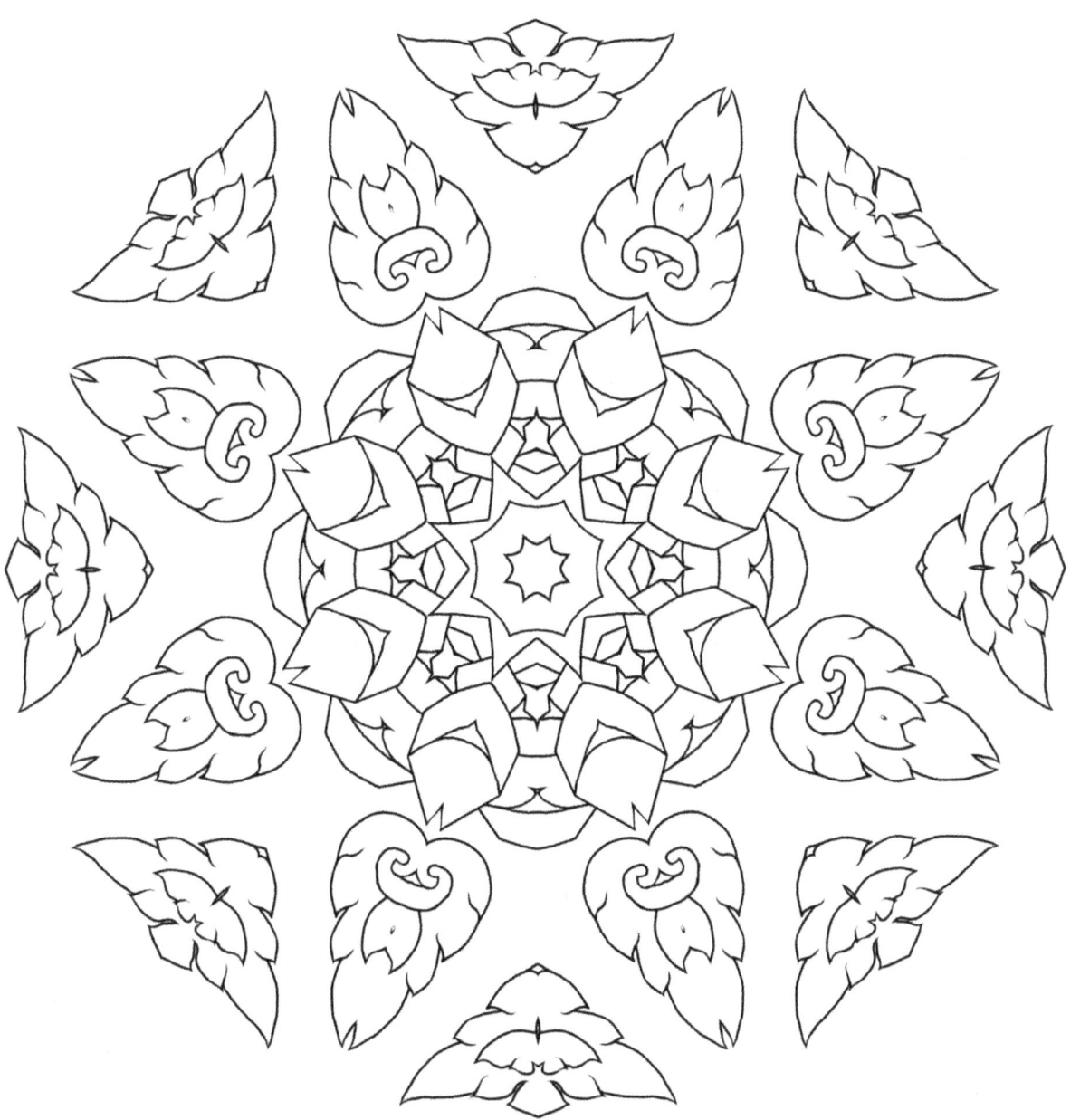

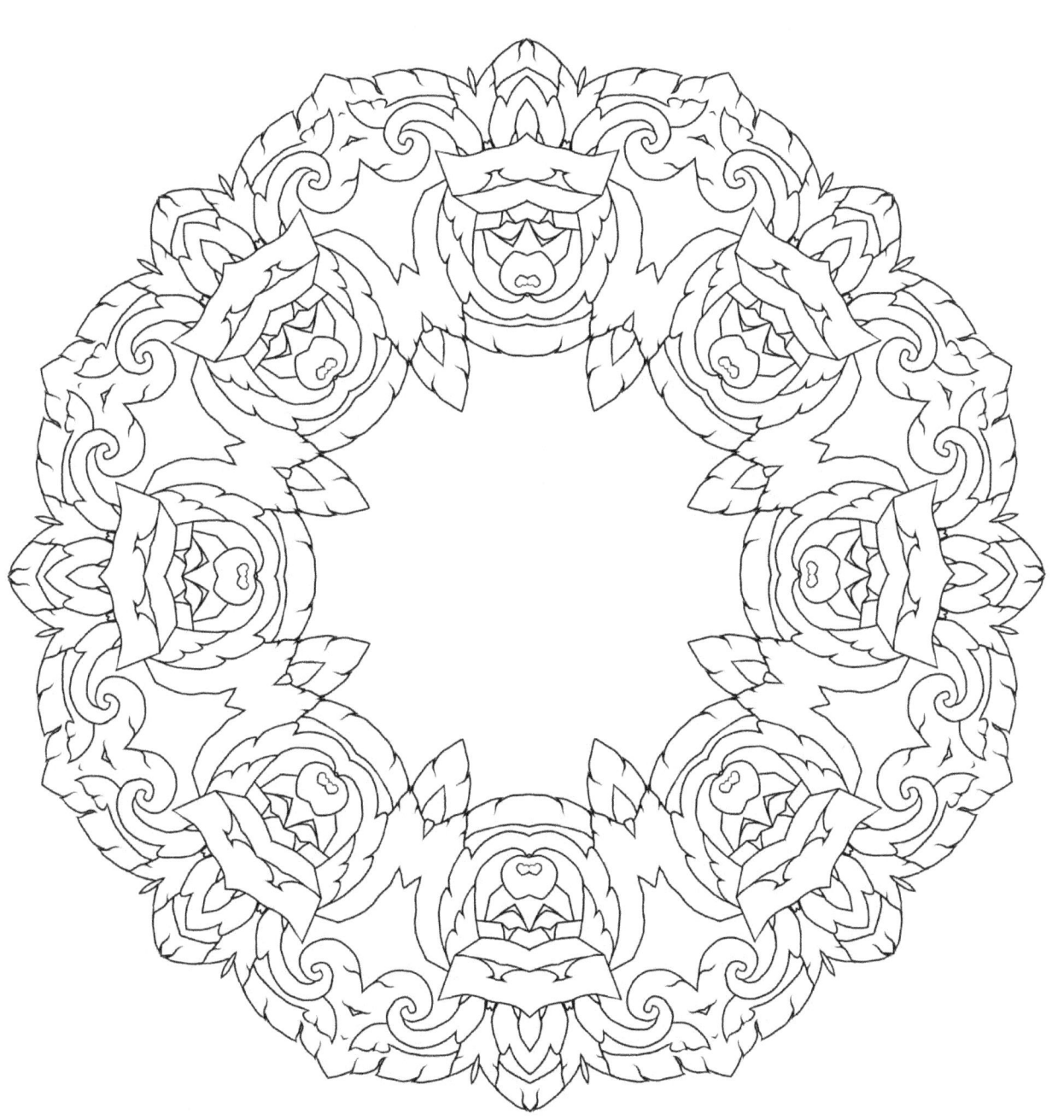

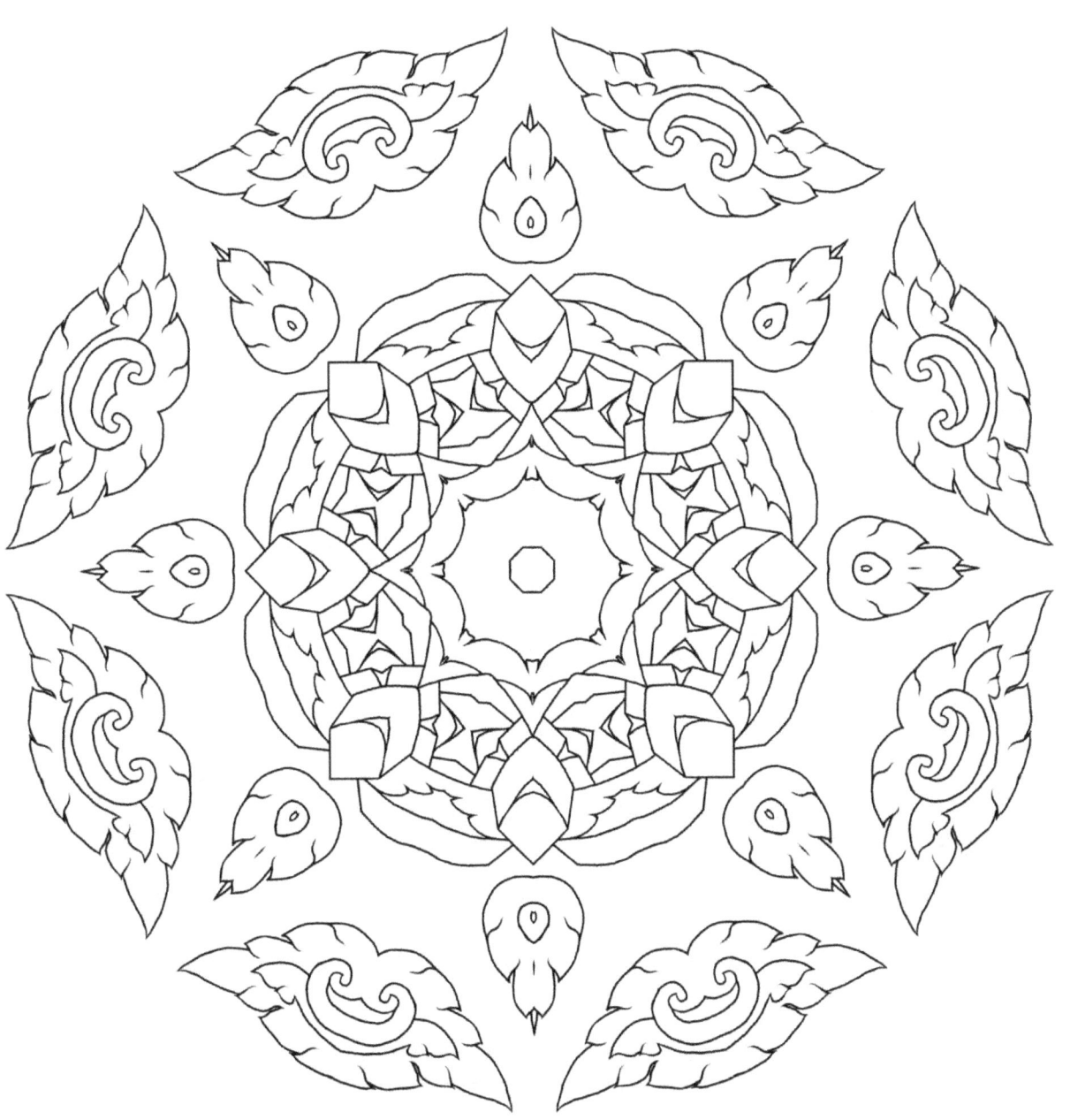

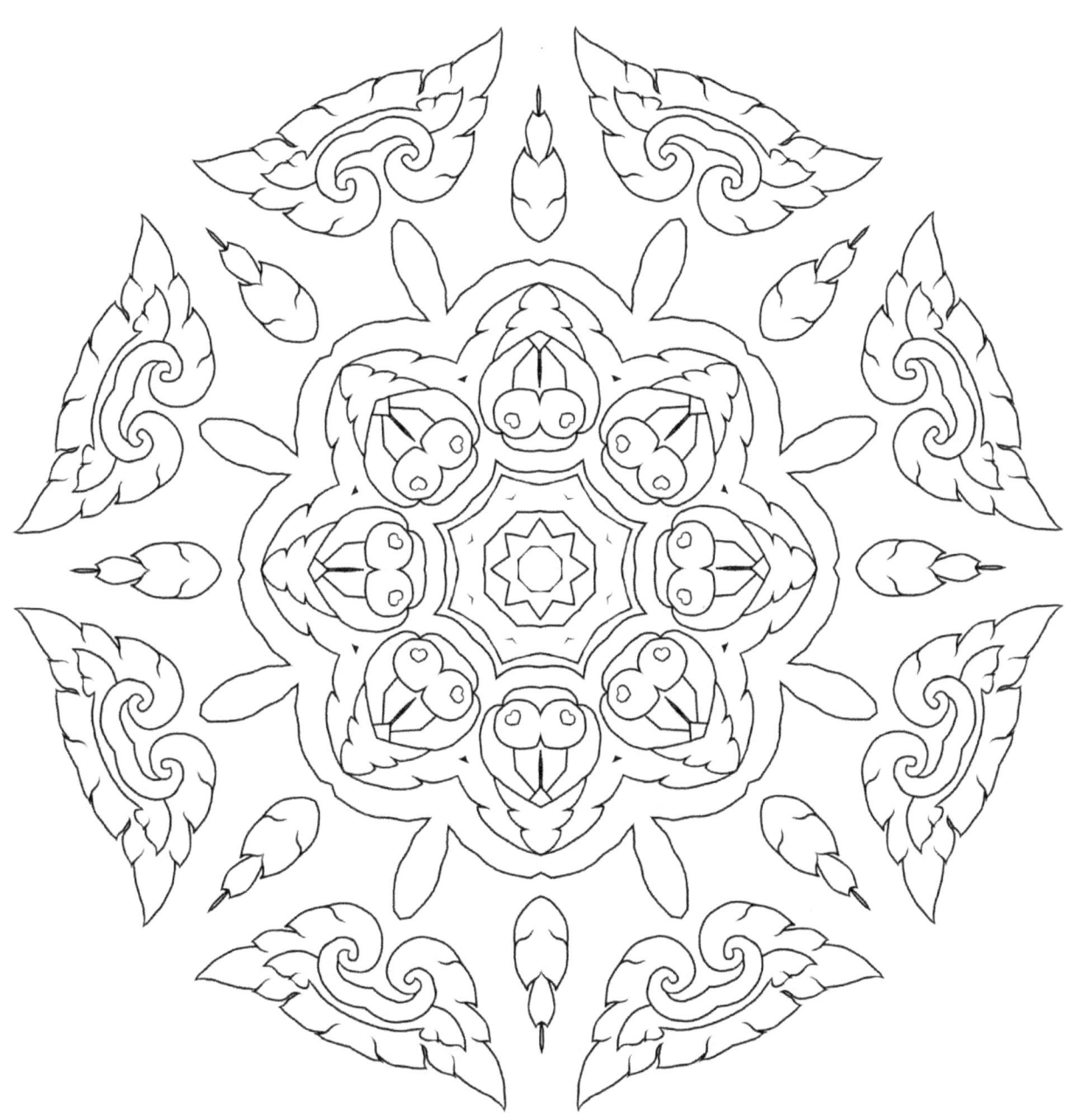

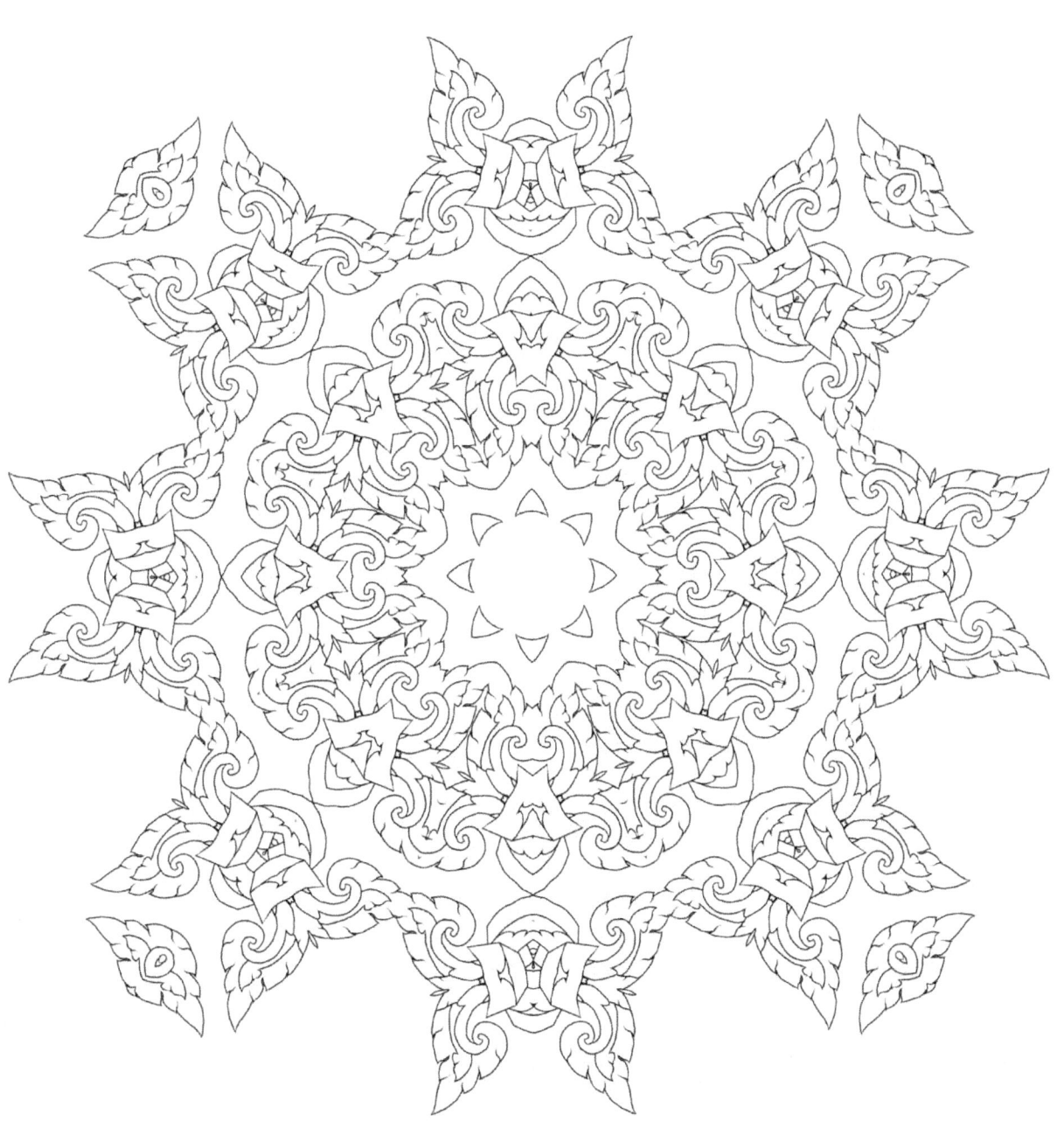

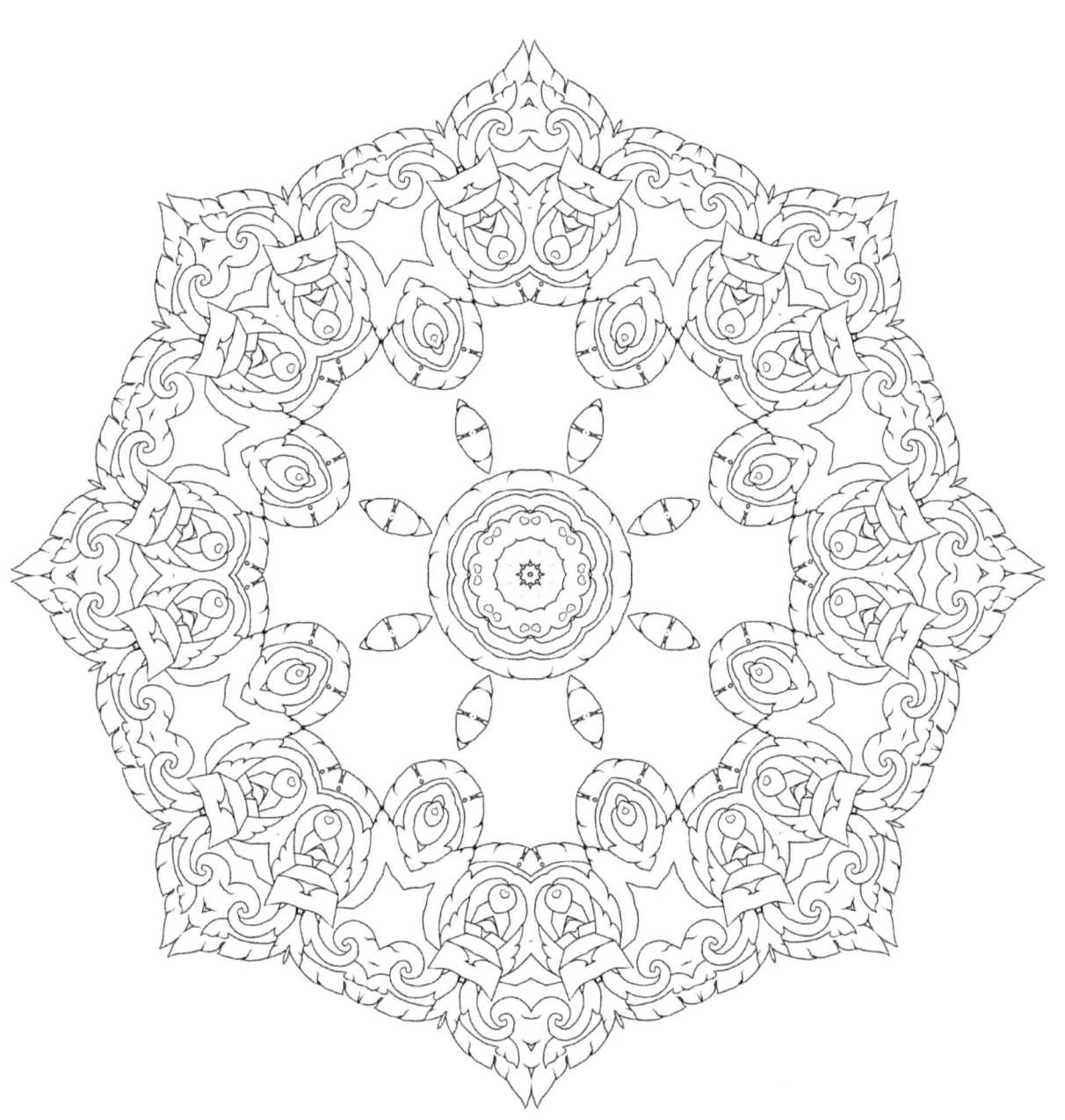

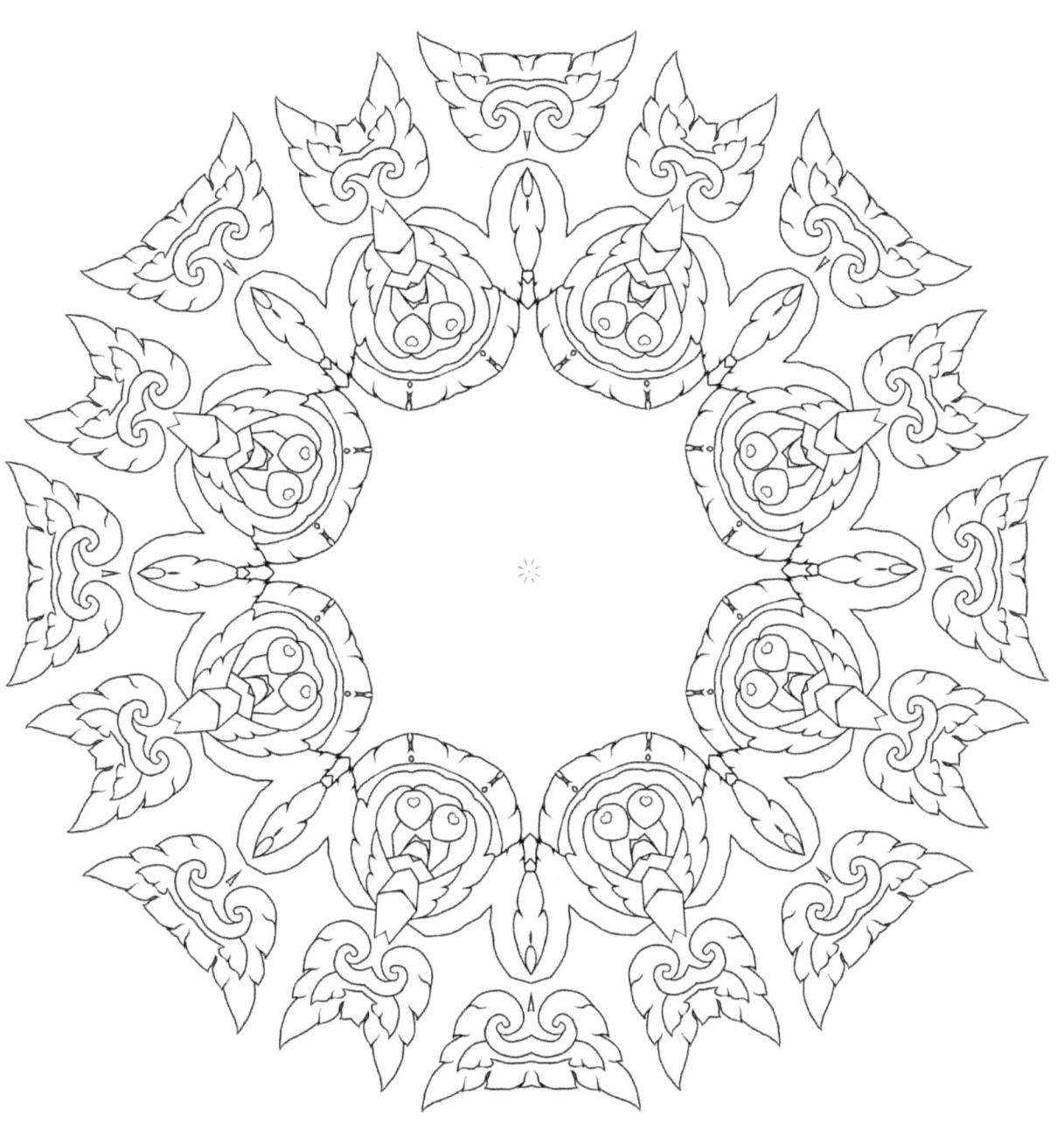

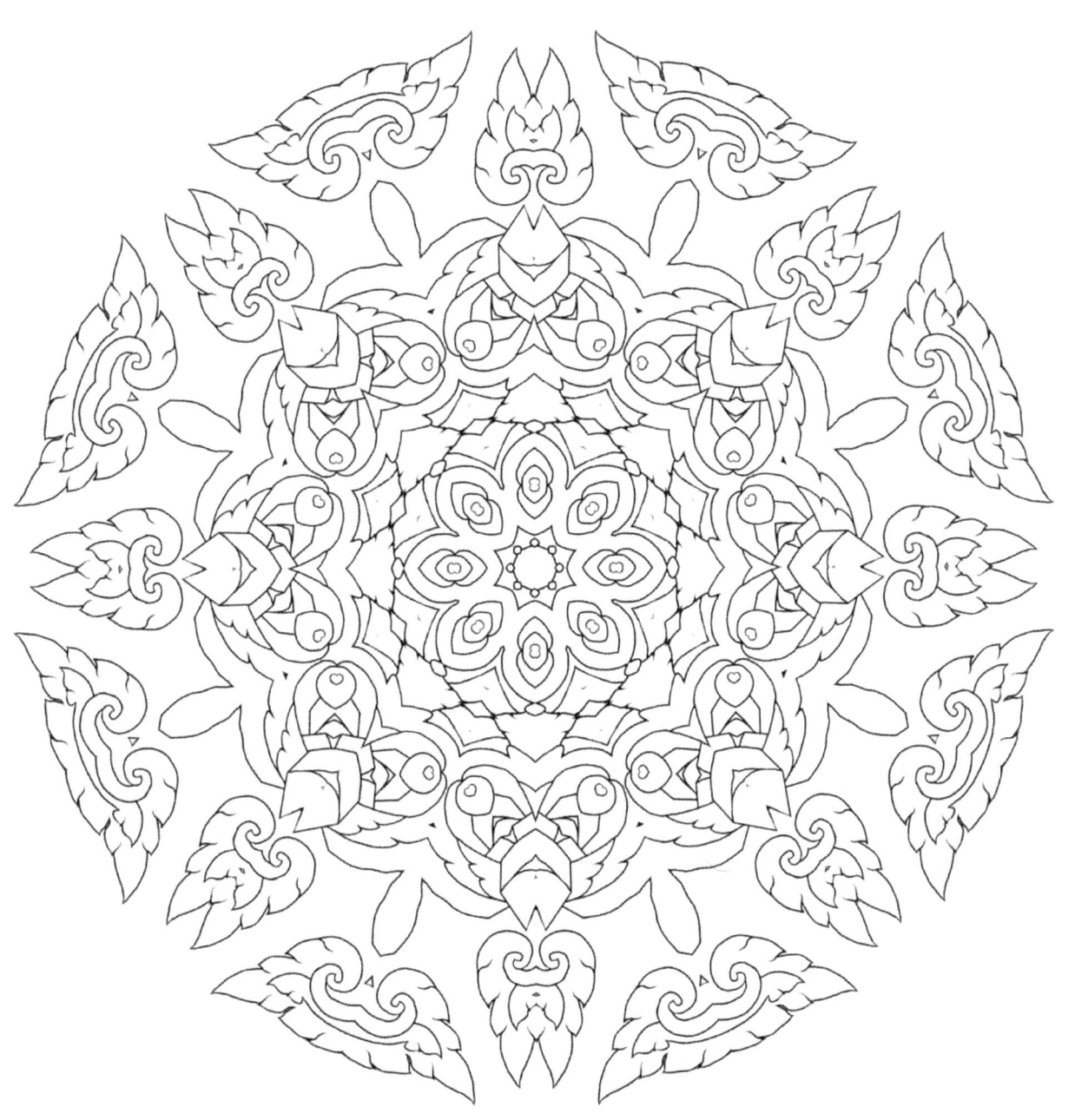

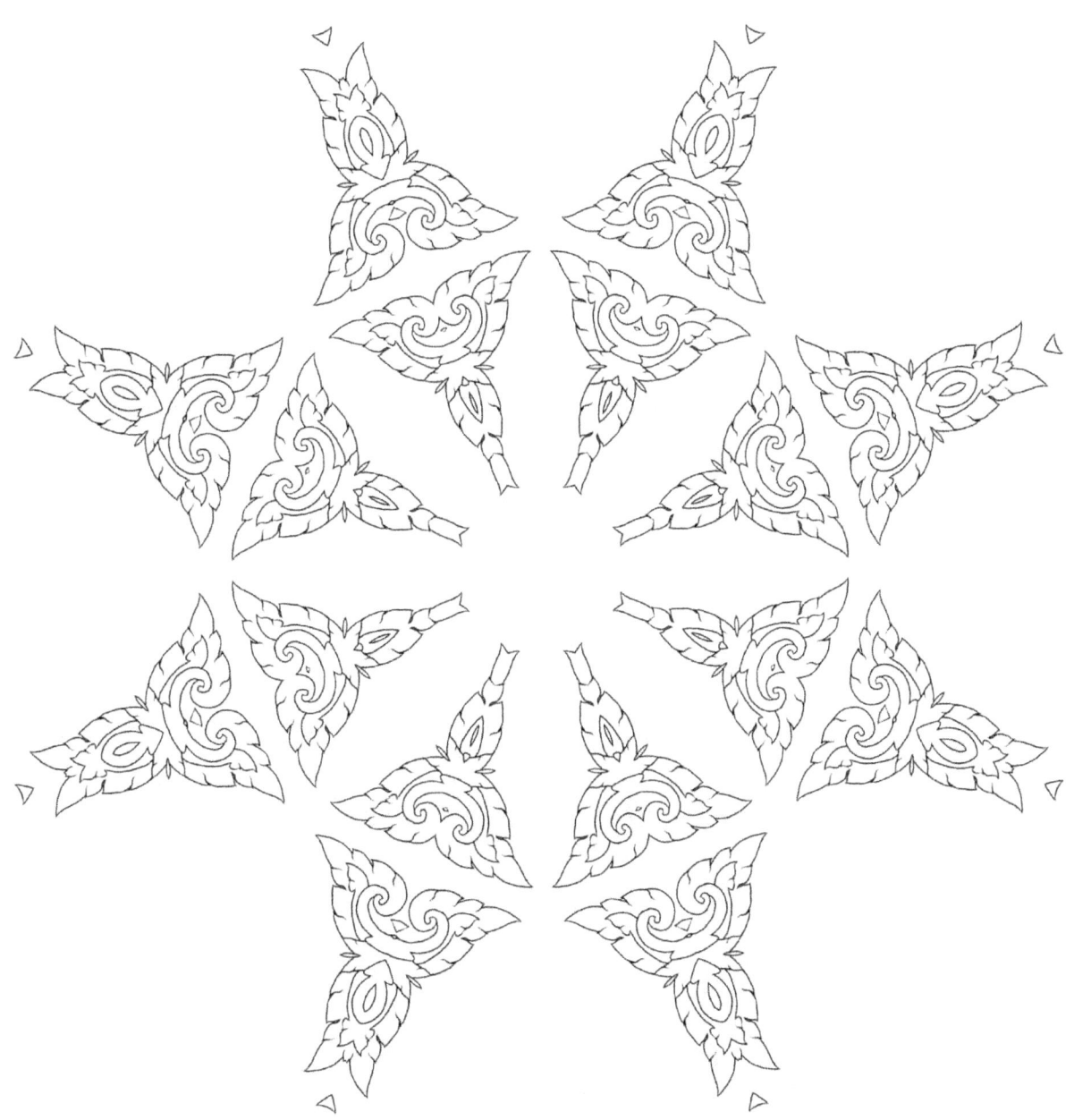

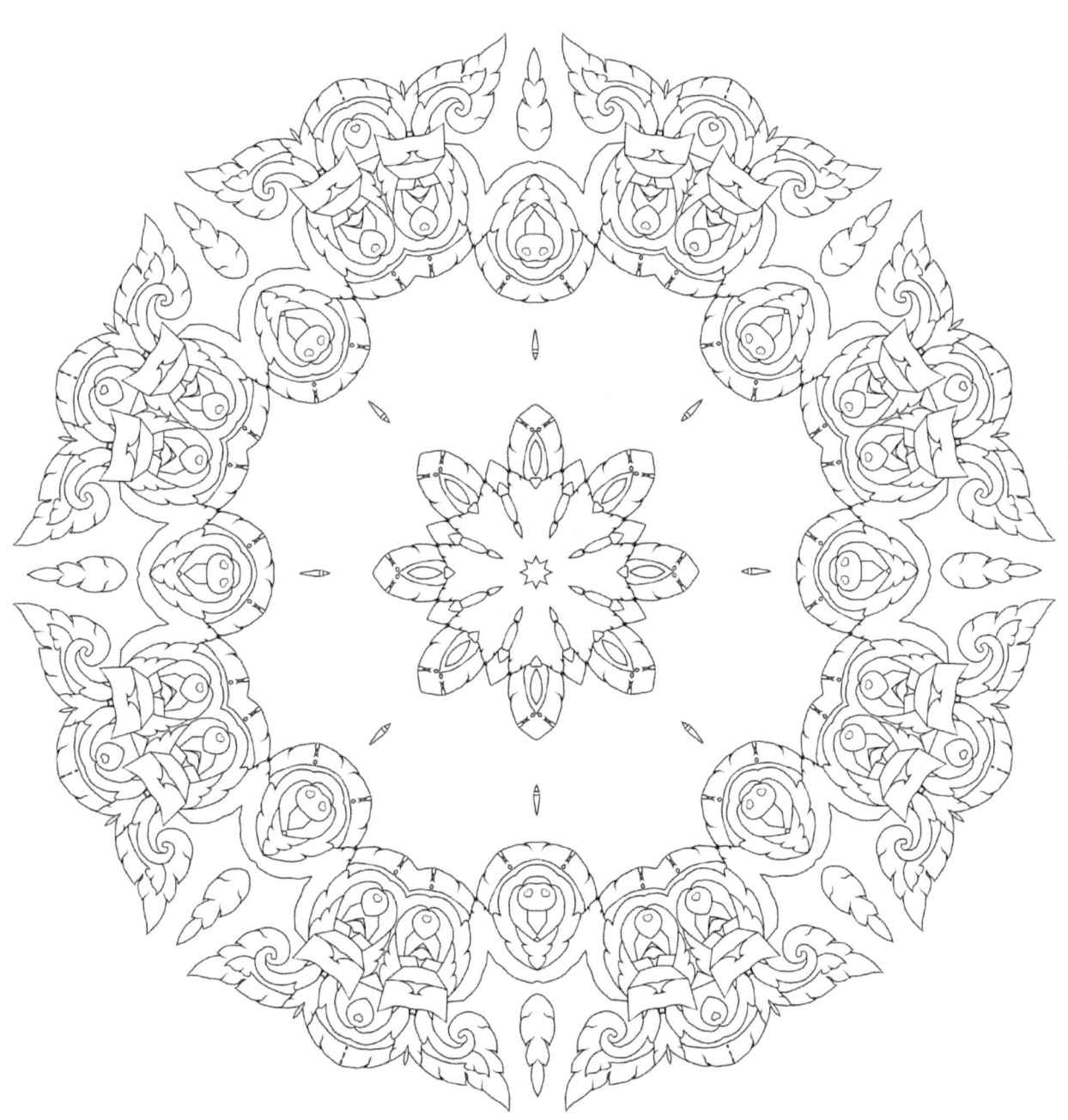

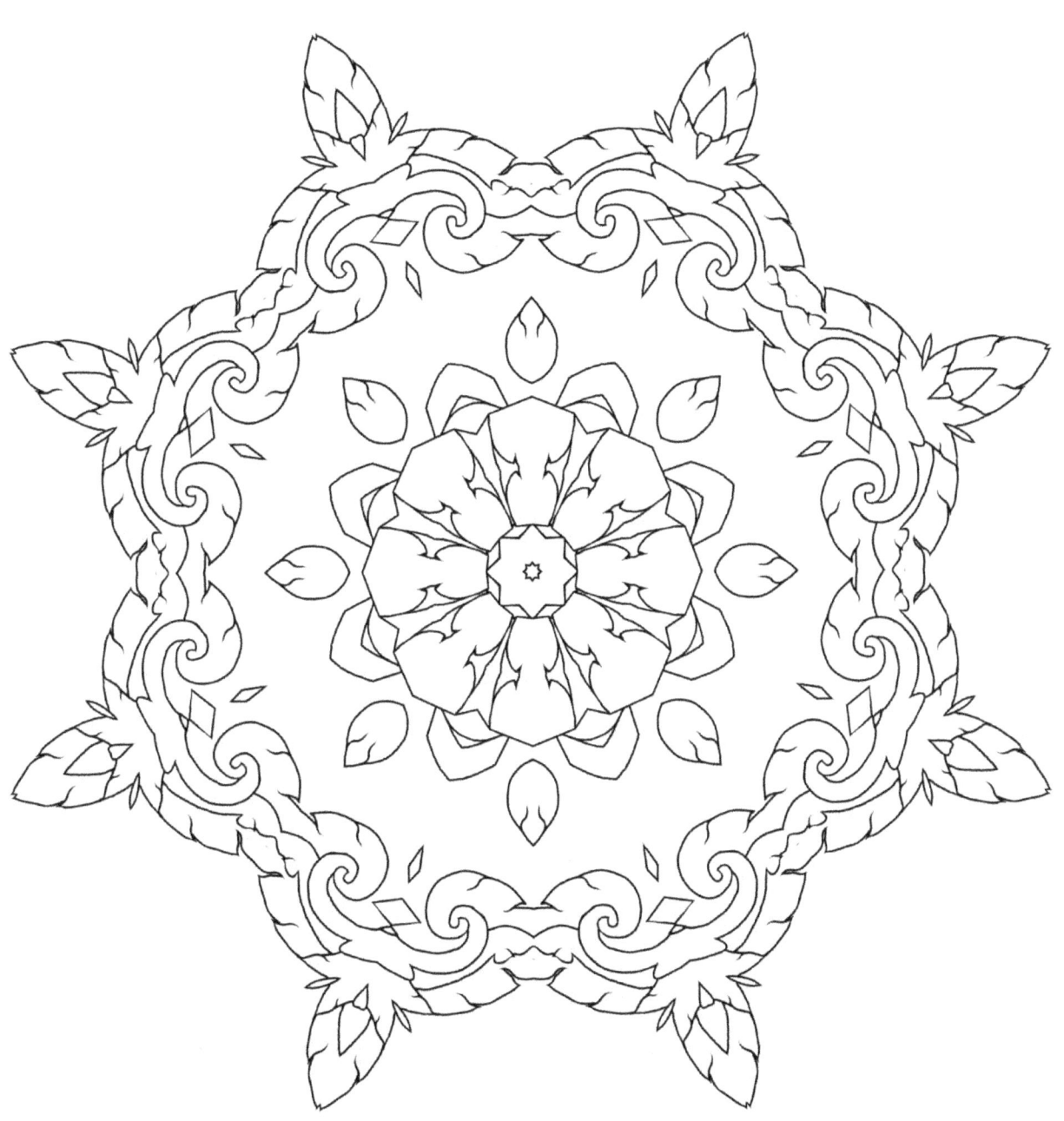

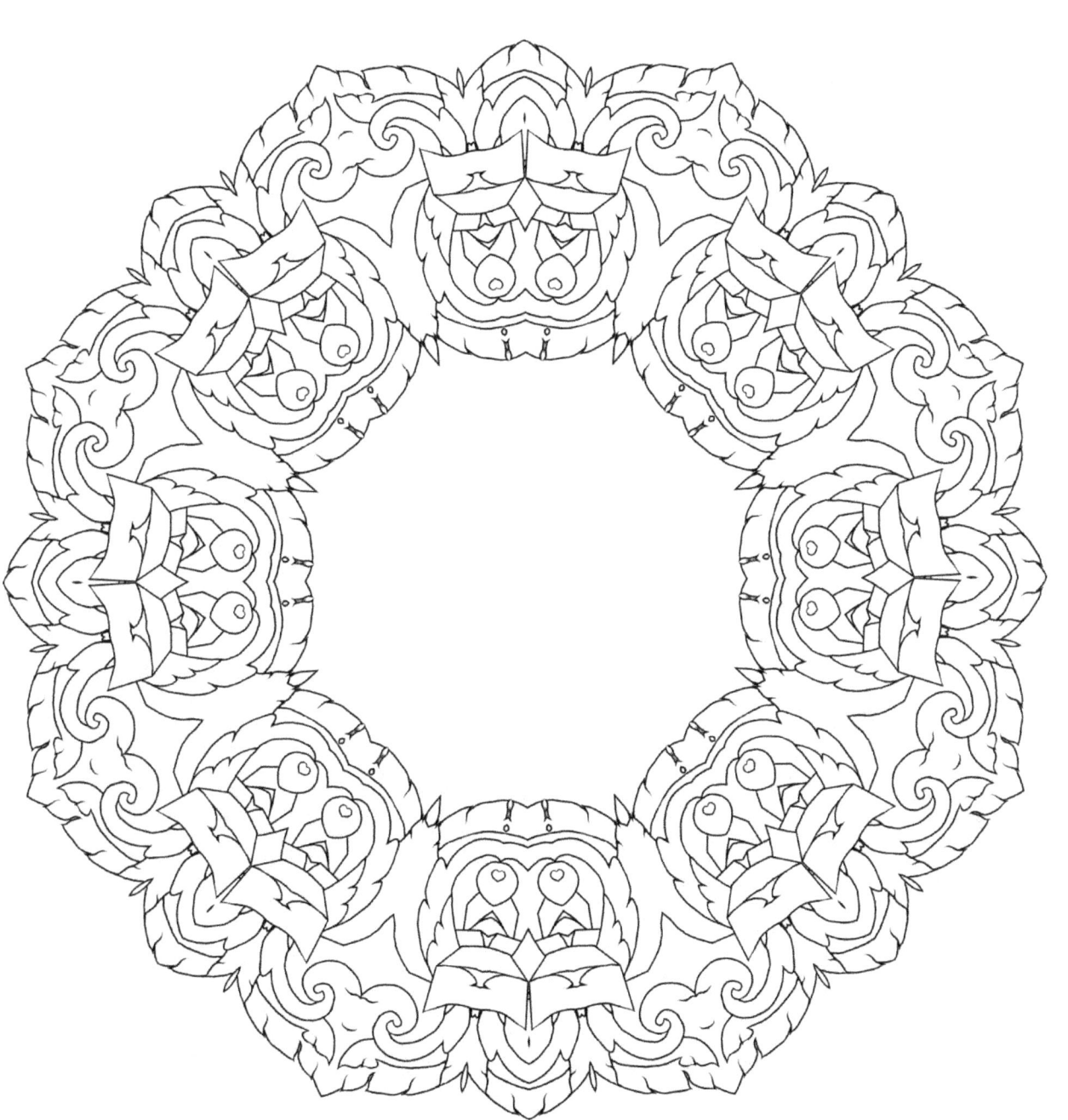

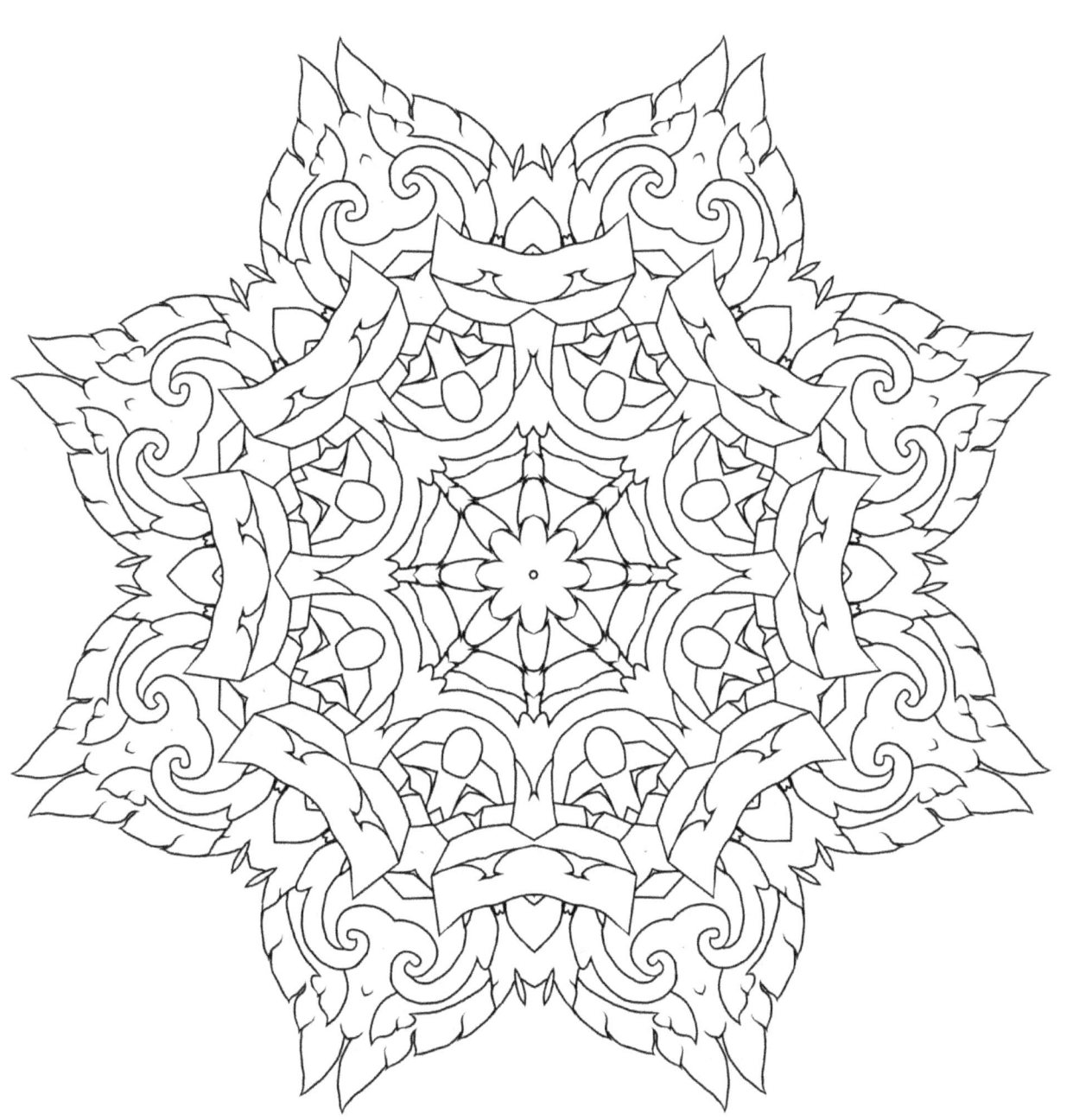

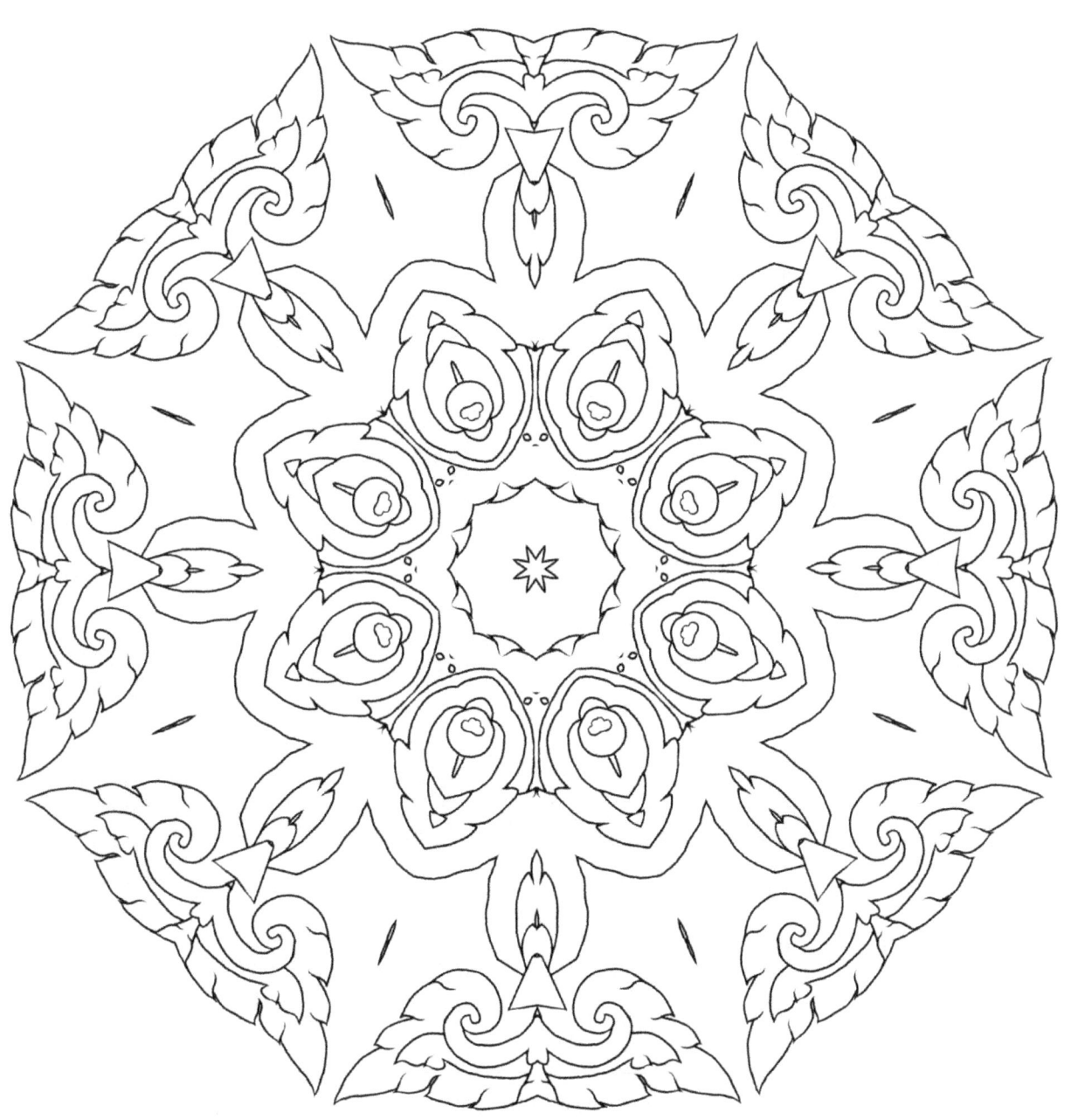

Thank you

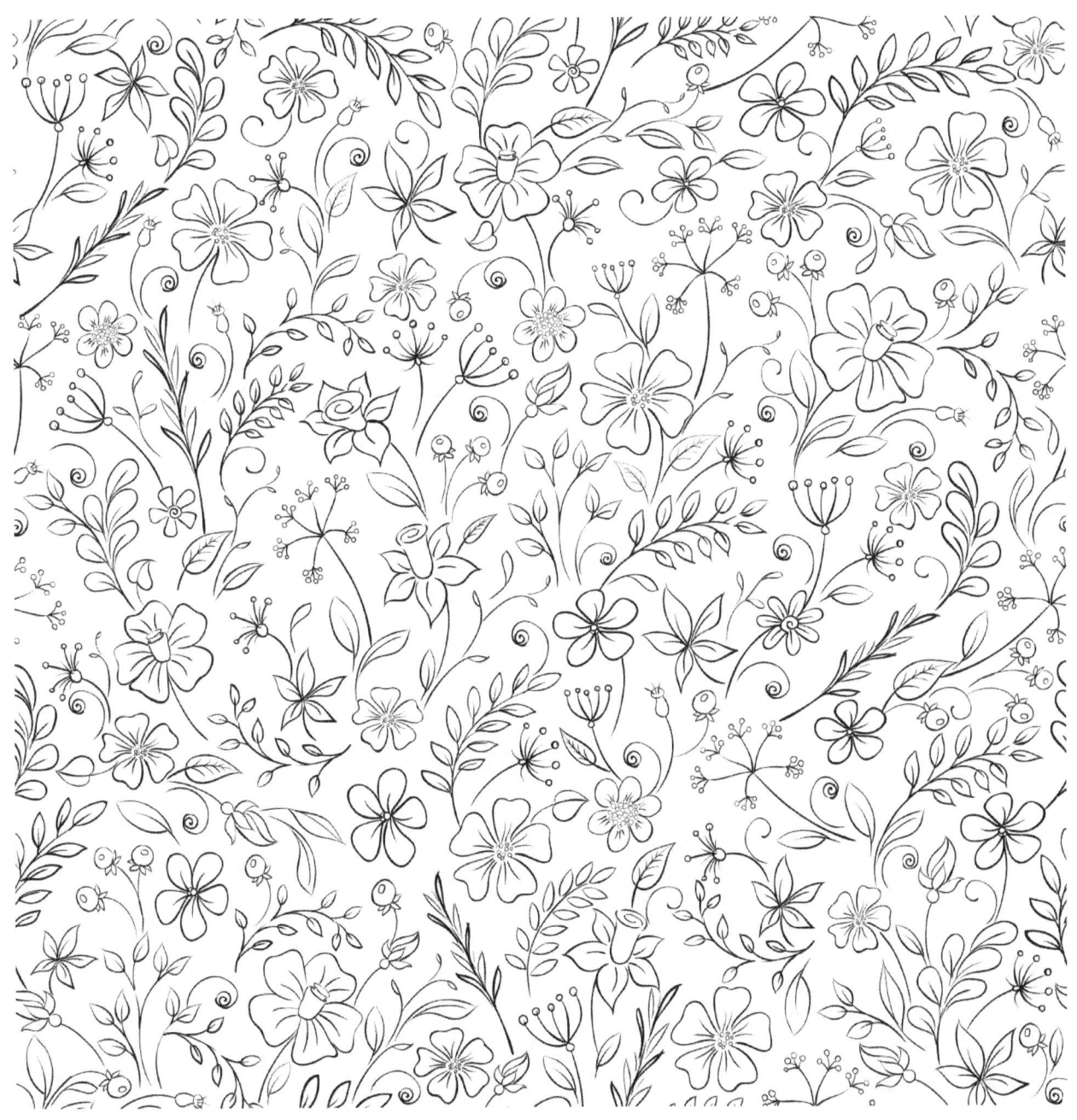

www.ingramcontent.com/pod-product-compliance
Lightning Source LLC
Chambersburg PA
CBHW081117180526

45170CB00008B/2893